The Complete

TOOLKIT

for building High-Performance

WORK
TEAMS

Nancy Golden

&

Joyce P. Gall

Clearinghouse on Educational Management
University of Oregon
2000

Golden, Nancy (Nancy L.)

The complete toolkit for building high-performance work teams /
Nancy Golden & Joyce P. Gall.

p. cm.

Includes bibliographical references (p.).

ISBN: 0-86552-144-1

1. School management teams. 2. School management and
organization. 3. Group decision making. I. Gall, Joyce P.
II. Title.

LB2806.3.G65   2000

371.2' 01--dc21

99-37661
CIP

Design: LeeAnn August

Type: 12/18 Times

Printer: University of Oregon Printing Department (GI60)

Printed in the United States of America, 2000

ERIC Clearinghouse on Educational Management

5207 University of Oregon
Eugene, OR 97403-5207
Telephone: (541) 346-5044 Fax: (541) 346-2334
World Wide Web: http://eric.uoregon.edu

This publication was prepared in part with funding from the Office of Educational Research and
Improvement, U.S. Department of Education, under contract no. ED-99-C0-0011. The opinions
expressed in this report do not necessarily reflect the positions or policies of the Department of
Education.

The University of Oregon is an equal opportunity, affirmative action institution committed to cultural
diversity.

MISSION OF ERIC
AND THE CLEARINGHOUSE

The Educational Resources Information Center (ERIC) is a national information system operated by the U.S. Department of Education. ERIC serves the educational community by disseminating research results and other resource information that can be used in developing more effective educational programs.

The ERIC Clearinghouse on Educational Management, one of several such units in the system, was established at the University of Oregon in 1966. The Clearinghouse and its companion units process research reports and journal articles for announcement in ERIC's index and abstract bulletins.

Research reports are announced in *Resources in Education* (*RIE*), available in many libraries and by subscription from the United States Government Printing Office, Washington, D.C. 20402-9371.

Most of the documents listed in *RIE* can be purchased through the ERIC Document Reproduction Service, operated by Cincinnati Bell Information Systems.

Journal articles are announced in *Current Index to Journals in Education. CIJE* is also available in many libraries and can be ordered from Oryx Press, 4041 North Central Avenue at Indian School, Suite 700, Phoenix, Arizona 85012. Semiannual cumulations can be ordered separately.

Besides processing documents and journal articles, the Clearinghouse prepares bibliographies, literature reviews, monographs, and other interpretive research studies on topics in its educational area.

CLEARINGHOUSE
NATIONAL ADVISORY BOARD

George Babigian, Executive Director, American Education Finance Association

Anne L. Bryant, Executive Director, National School Boards Association

Vincent Ferrandino, Executive Director, National Association of Elementary School Principals

Paul Houston, Executive Director, American Association of School Administrators

John T. MacDonald, Director, State Leadership Center, Council of Chief State School Officers

Philip K. Piele (Chair), Professor and Director, ERIC Clearinghouse on Educational Management, University of Oregon

Karen Seashore-Louis, Vice-President, Division A, American Educational Research Association

Gerald Tirozzi, Executive Director, National Association of Secondary School Principals

Michelle Young, Executive Director, University Council for Educational Administration

ADMINISTRATIVE STAFF

Philip K. Piele, Professor and Director

Stuart C. Smith, Associate Director

Preface

The Complete Toolkit for Building High-Performance Work Teams is meant to empower both the leaders and the members of work teams in educational and social-service systems. It presents, in a simple yet systematic fashion, a set of tested facilitation tools that will help teams (a) work more efficiently and harmoniously to achieve their goals, (b) deal directly with both personal and work-related issues that might otherwise disrupt or hamper the progress of the teams, and (c) make their work a more lively, enjoyable, and growth-producing learning experience. From direct experience we know that these tools can help teams accomplish their mission, whatever the teams' size, composition, structure, or desired outcomes.

The Toolkit began as a number of tools that the first author, Nancy Golden, learned from professional colleagues, discovered in the educational literature, or designed herself to aid her in serving as a facilitator for various teams and committees working on major tasks and issues in the field of education. As a district administrator Golden was called on to provide leadership for many such groups. Her long experience as a public school teacher, administrator, parent, and community member convinced her that the best form of leadership is to facilitate interactions among participants and draw them into the process of decision-making and consensus-building.

From direct experience we know that these tools can help teams accomplish their mission, whatever the teams' size, composition, structure, or desired outcomes.

In 1994 Golden, while working in the Albany School District as the deputy superintendent responsible for curriculum, produced a document that included twelve facilitation tools she used extensively to build high-performance work teams in her own and other school districts. As director of the Administrator Licensure Program at the University of Oregon since 1997, Golden continued using those tools with both university and school groups and perceived a need to make them more widely available to educational and social-service system leaders.

Preface

Joyce (Joy) Gall, the second author, has developed curriculum materials and coauthored books in education for many years. As a social psychologist concerned with group functioning and leadership, she helped provide context and organizational structure for the facilitation tools, thereby enhancing their effectiveness for preparing professionals for team membership or leadership and making them accessible to a wider audience.

The tools in this booklet have been refined for clarity, expanded to seventeen in number, and organized by the phase of group life when each is likely to be most useful. We have also added real-life examples of the tools in use.

We know that all the members of a team teach and lead one another at different points in time. Thus we invite readers to become part of our teaching-learning team and to send us feedback, positive or negative, on this Toolkit so that we may continue to improve it. Please contact us at the Administrator Licensure Program, College of Education, 5267 University of Oregon, Eugene, OR 97403-5267; call Nancy at (541) 346-1308 or email her at <nlgolden@oregon.uoregon.edu>; or call Joy at (541) 346-5185 or email her at <joygall@oregon.uoregon.edu>.

Nancy Golden, Ph.D.
Joyce P. Gall, Ph.D.

About the Administrator Licensure Program

The Administrator Licensure Program at the University of Oregon provides preparation for initial and continuing licensure of school administrators and for licensure of superintendents. Recently restructured, the program uses a design-and-delivery model based on the sensed need for new conceptions of leadership and new approaches to the preparation of educational leaders.

The program integrates theory and practice through collaborative teaching by university faculty and practitioners, students' completion of a field-based practicum, and the development of mentor relationships between program participants and experienced practitioners. The program also uses a cohort model in which students newly admitted to each licensure program participate as a group in instructional institutes and other university-based activities.

School administrators must seek better ways to involve a variety of stakeholders in the planning, design, and implementation of school-improvement efforts.

The program strives to keep pace with the continual stream of discoveries and changes involving the organization and administration of educational systems. As an example of such discoveries, the education literature clearly shows that when individuals participate in creating an innovation they are much more likely to follow through in implementing and maintaining the new procedures and commitments that it entails. Thus school administrators must seek better ways to involve a variety of stakeholders in the planning, design, and implementation of school-improvement efforts.

Examples of changes in the structure of schools include the development of site councils that participate in school decision-making, and the rise of collaborative partnerships between schools and community agencies such as major employers. These structural changes have brought many individuals having little or no formal preparation in educational administration into shared-leadership roles in the schools.

These examples reveal that school leadership is no longer the exclusive responsibility of building and central-office administrators. Instead, school administrators perceive a growing need to involve both teaching and service professionals and community representatives in order to reach agreement, or workable compromise, on the mission and operation of the schools they serve.

Preparation in a new form of leadership, called facilitative leadership, will help future administrators work more effectively with the great variety and number of individuals who participate in work teams for schools and other social-service organizations serving youth and adult learners. This Toolkit is designed to help participants in the University of Oregon Administrator Licensure Program, as well as administrators in educational and social-service systems generally, learn—and in turn help others learn—how to provide this form of leadership.

Table of Contents

Table of Contents

Building High-Performance Work Teams: Well Worth the Effort

As an educational leader, you probably spend considerable time facilitating the work of varied types of teams. Whether chairing a school staff or board meeting, leading an ad hoc educational task force, or helping a group of students plan a fund-raiser, the biggest challenge to the team leader often involves keeping the team moving forward, toward consensus on needed action steps.

Perhaps you have attended the team meeting from hell: Time dragged for an hour or more, some people griped or criticized, others seemed to be hiding tension or perhaps not even listening, and very little was accomplished. When you leave such a meeting, relief at finally being free is often mixed with a nagging sense that important issues remain unresolved, that opposing viewpoints have set the stage for group conflict, or that people left without making commitments to take action or even knowing what actions are needed to move the team forward.

Goals for the Toolkit

The facilitation tools in this booklet will help you build high-performance work teams—teams that focus on determining actions needed to achieve team goals and reaching sufficient agreement for taking those actions. Using these tools will help you achieve three key goals:

1. *Increasing your skills as a team leader.* The nature of educational leadership is undergoing change. Jerry Patterson (1993) points out five key value areas that are typical of what he calls "tomorrow's" organization, namely, openness to participation, openness to diversity, openness to conflict, openness to reflection, and openness to mistakes. This change of values, now under way, calls for a dramatic shift in the way that groups and organizations need to be led in order to achieve their mission. To highlight these shifts, Patterson contrasts typical signs of strength and weakness in what he calls "today's" and "tomorrow's" organization.

Here we describe these strengths and weaknesses as how things have been in the past versus how they will be in the future, with the present representing the shift that is occurring. In the past, indicators that "everything's under control" were interpreted as signs of strength, while indicators of "everything's up for grabs" were interpreted as signs of weakness. By contrast, in the future, the desired scenario is almost the exact opposite: A situation in which "everything's on the table" will be seen as a sign of strength, and a situation in which "everything's controlled" will be seen as a sign of weakness. To lead work teams, therefore, you must be able to effectively help individuals embrace these shifts in values and behavior, perhaps while still going through them yourself.

This Toolkit is meant for any of the types of people who commonly serve as team leaders or facilitators. You might be an administrator or staff member with overall responsibility for the outcome of the team's work. If so, these tools will show team members and others in your organization your commitment to practicing facilitative leadership rather than top-down control (Conley & Goldman, 1994). If you are an outside consultant, use of these tools will promote your credibility and help you build a common language and process for guiding the work team. Or perhaps you are a team member who has volunteered or been recruited to serve as team leader. The tools provide a clear structure and guidelines for leadership that can be used even by individuals who are not typically "in charge."

2. *Energizing and improving the performance of any educational or social-service-system team with which you work.* Every member of educational and social-service organizations must understand the key role they can and indeed must play in their groups and organizations in order for the change we have described to move forward rather than be hindered. Therefore, leadership can no longer be treated as a rare personal quality nor as a plum reserved for the chosen few; instead it must be shared and spread throughout every group and organization.

Many groups and individuals are calling for a variety of changes in the educational system. As Michael Fullan and Suzanne Stiegelbauer (1991) point out:

...no matter how honorable the motives, each and every individual

who is necessary for effective implementation will experience some concerns about the meaning of new practices, goals, beliefs, and means of implementation. The presence or absence of mechanisms to address the ongoing problem of meaning—at the beginning and as people try out ideas—is crucial for success, because it is at the individual level that change does or does not occur (p. 45).

The Toolkit helps individuals and teams grapple with the problem of the meaning of change. We intend it to foster collaborative decision-making throughout educational and social-service systems. It is designed to help prepare participants for making proactive contributions and assuming leadership roles as they carry out

> **We intend this Toolkit to help foster collaborative decision-making throughout educational and social-service systems.**

their jobs or perform service in their communities. For this reason, we recommend that you make a photocopy set of the tool cards contained in this Toolkit for each member of the teams with which you work. If team members have access to the tool cards, and if you explain your reasons for using particular tools in various situations, team members will be more likely to accept and contribute to the processes that you employ to move the team forward.

3. *Preparing other team leaders.* In the future, every participant in a group or organization may be expected to provide leadership at various points in time. Part of the shift occurring in leadership involves a recognition that learning often occurs best by doing—in other words, individuals learn to lead by practicing leadership in real-life contexts.

Using the tools in this booklet with work teams will enable you to actively prepare other team members for serving as team leaders. If you want to increase the work team's emphasis on preparing team leaders, we suggest you inform the team of this goal. You might also indicate that when appropriate you will encourage volunteers to cofacilitate certain team activities with you or to facilitate activities on their own. Some suggestions for preparing other team leaders are provided after the tools have been presented.

Key Tools for Facilitating Work Teams

The 17 tools provided in this booklet are clustered into three phases that are evident in the functioning of many teams: (1) laying the groundwork, (2) working toward consensus, and (3) moving into action. Each tool will help you move your team through these phases. However, it is perfectly appropriate for you to use the tools in a different order, or to choose to use some tools and not others, depending on your team structure and purpose at any given point.

Each tool is presented in detail, beginning with a summary of *what* the tool involves, *when* it is appropriate to use the tool, and *why* that tool will help move a team forward. We also outline steps for using each tool and give an example of how it has helped real teams in educational and social-service settings reach agreements on the actions needed to move forward.

For your convenience, the key guidelines for using each tool are listed on a set of 5-1/2" X 8-1/2" tool cards. As issues arise, team members can use the tool cards to assist them in applying the appropriate tool to address specific needs and challenges. One set of tool cards, for the team leader's use, is in the envelope at the back of the Toolkit.

At the end of the Toolkit you will find a set of reproducible masters of the tool cards, printed two to an 8-1/2" X 11" page, which you can use to make copies of the tool cards for each member of the work team.

Phase I. Laying the Groundwork

Laying the groundwork is critical to team success. For example, many teachers do not try to teach much content during the first week of school; instead they devote considerable class time to establishing classroom-management procedures. Similarly, professional work teams need a structure and some ground rules before they can work together smoothly and effectively.

Before you begin using any of the tools, be sure all the routine matters necessary for the team's functioning are in place. They include reviewing or establishing the mission of the organization or larger entity (e.g., a school district) to which the team's work is meant to contribute.

Here we will summarize a few general strategies for facilitating work teams, before introducing the five tools in this section.

Concluding Small-Group Activities

This Toolkit includes various small-group activities intended to help team members have fun and keep their energy level high while carrying out productive thinking and group discussion. Because meeting time is usually at a premium, the team leader needs to enlist team members' help in bringing the team back together promptly after each activity so it can keep moving forward.

We recommend that you collect a few noisemakers that you can use to stop conversation and get everyone's attention when you are ready to announce the next activity or agenda item—a whistle, toy horn or drum, kitchen timer, etc. You might also want to use props, such as a hardhat or feather boa, to get the team's attention back on you. Such props are effective and fun if the team is receptive, but they may backfire otherwise. You need to assess the team's receptivity to various types of facilitation strategies, and use whatever works to keep things moving.

To refocus team members' attention it also helps to use simple phrases that signal a shift in team activity and require a specific response from all team members. For example, you could say "When the hand goes up, the mouth goes shut," meaning that whenever you raise your hand you expect everyone to stop talking and listen for the next direction. Or to get the group's attention when people are talking loudly, you could say, in a voice with volume, "Help me out!" Such a phrase appeals to most team members' sense of joint responsibility for ensuring a productive meeting.

Explaining the Decision-Making Process

Depending on your normal responsibilities in the group or organization, you might want to explain your own and other team members' role in the work team's decision making. If you serve regularly as an in-house leader, you are likely to have responsibilities beyond those of other team members that will affect your actions and decisions in the team. You might wish to explain how any disagreements will be resolved, e.g., by majority vote, by your exercising tie-breaking authority when necessary, or by your having the final say. Or you might want to say something like, "Depending on the situation, we'll make some decisions collaboratively, some I'll make after asking for input from all of you, and some decisions I'll make on my own."

This section presents five tools that will help you lay the groundwork to foster the effective functioning of any team for which you serve as facilitator.

- **Tool 1,** *State a Purpose* helps a team state its overall purpose, set goals for each meeting, and clarify new or changing goals as they emerge.

- **Tool 2,** *Set Group Agreements* establishes the ground rules for team decision-making and provides guidelines for how team members should interact.

- **Tool 3,** *Develop a Common Knowledge Base* is designed to help the team obtain and share the knowledge it needs as a basis for its work.

- **Tool 4,** *Clarify Consensus* helps a team understand the meaning of consensus and the role it can play in effective team functioning.

- **Tool 5,** *Form Kaleidoscope Groups* illustrates the value of members engaging in indepth communication with other members who have different stakes or perspectives regarding key issues of concern.

Tool 1. State a Purpose

What: *State a Purpose* is a process to help the team clarify its specific goal and the priorities that determine its focus.

When: Use *State a Purpose* at the first team meeting to help all team members start their work together "on the same page," and at subsequent meetings to help team members focus on their most important priorities at particular points in time.

Why: Often members bring very different assumptions and goals to a work team. This process helps to ensure that the team has enough common ground to blend or choose among those goals as it carries out its work.

Process for Stating a Purpose

1. At the initial team meeting point out that being clear and specific about the team's purpose helps keep team members on track and helps the team achieve its purpose in a timely way.

2. Give examples of the specific purpose of work teams with which you have been affiliated (e.g., to develop a school program to reduce student failure), or of individual team meetings (e.g., to review school data on student dropout rates).

3. Ask members to share their views as to the team's overall purpose. If there is disagreement you may wish to use **Tool 6,** *Fly the Helicopter Higher* or **Tool 8,** *Ask Yes-No-What Do You Need?* to achieve consensus on the team's purpose.

4. At each subsequent meeting, ask someone to state the purpose of the meeting, that is, the outcome to be achieved by the end of the meeting that indicates the meeting was effective.

Setting Priorities on the Goals of a Team Meeting

1. To help members stay on task, list the varied goals that they are trying to accomplish, and note those that differ sufficiently on a chart pad.

2. By rating each goal from 1 (low) to 5 (high) on both its urgency and its importance, team members set priorities and maintain team focus.

    a. The *importance* of a particular goal signifies how critical it is to achievement of the team's overall purpose.

    b. The *urgency* of a particular goal signifies how critical it is that the goal be achieved now instead of later.

3. The importance and urgency scores provided by each team member are added together and the total score for each goal is calculated.

Clarifying the Team's Purpose

A team of school teachers from the Peppertown School District met periodically to develop plans for aligning the school curriculum with a set of student learning standards that the state legislature had established. As their alignment plan took shape, the team began sensing various needs for the district's teachers to receive preparation (that is, training) in order to provide the aligned curriculum to students and assess its effectiveness.

State a Purpose

The team leader then suggested that one or more subsequent meetings be devoted to identifying preparation needs and planning for how they could be met. Reminding team members of this goal helped ensure a focus on preparation needs and plans during the team's next meeting.

Tool 2. Set Group Agreements

What: Setting group agreements is a process for clarifying the general behavior that team members can count on from each other, and establishing the ground rules for how the team will make decisions and handle conflict.

When: If possible, set group agreements at the first team meeting.

Why: A team functions much more comfortably and efficiently if members understand what they can expect and what is expected of them.

Process for Setting Group Agreements

1. During team meetings people should feel free to take care of their personal needs, like getting a cup of coffee or using the restroom. Suggest that everyone agree to follow the 21-year-old rule, that is, "We're all adults, and we'll act that way" in taking care of personal needs in a way that minimizes disruptions to the meeting.

2. Ask members to brainstorm a list of the characteristics of the ineffective meetings they've attended, and write it on chart pack paper. Then ask them to list the characteristics of effective meetings.

3. Using the lists as a basis, ask team members to volunteer ideas for specific agreements needed to ensure effective team functioning. You may wish to suggest topics to address (e.g., attendance, agenda, minutes, meeting tasks, tasks between meetings, decision-making, handling conflict).

4. Coach the members who introduce ideas to say precisely what they need from the group, and how agreement about it will promote individuals' comfort and the team's effectiveness. If no one says anything contradictory, you can accept all these needs as group agreements.

5. In cases of disagreement, have members discuss differing viewpoints. You may wish to use one or more of the tools from Phase II Working toward Consensus to help the team reach consensus on group agreements.

6. Ask someone to type up the group agreements and make copies for each team member. Emphasize that you expect all team members to follow all the group agreements, and if they want to change any of them in the future to bring it up for discussion at a future meeting.

7. In subsequent meetings, if you sense someone is not following the group agreements, remind team members of the relevant agreement and their commitment to follow it.

Developing Group Agreements

The following example illustrates agreements reached by the advisory board for a school-based family resource center based at Wilson Elementary School.

1. *Decision-Making.* **Decisions will be made by consensus whenever possible. If consensus cannot be reached, a decision has not been made. If a deadline for a decision is upcoming, the decision will be made by a quorum of team members. A quorum is defined as one**

more than half of the total number of voting members. If a quorum is not present at a meeting, a decision can be made by doing a phone or e-mail survey of voting members.

2. *Voting Members.* Those attending team meetings may include others besides voting members. For this center, voting members include all the members of the center's advisory board and supervisors of the center staff, while nonvoting members are the members of the center staff.

3. *Meeting Responsibilities.* Individuals will volunteer to carry out various responsibilities at each team meeting. If more than one individual volunteers for a given responsibility, it can be shared, or team members can vote on which individual they want to perform that responsibility. Responsibilities include meeting facilitator, recorder, and timekeeper, and others may be added as the need emerges.

4. *Agenda.* Any team member can propose items for the next meeting's agenda. A copy of the agenda will be available at the beginning of each team meeting, and members may add items at that time.

5. *Minutes.* Minutes of the previous meeting will be read at the beginning of each team meeting. Members can make corrections or additions and then vote to approve the minutes if desired.

6. *Attendance.* All team members agree to attend every meeting, or to notify the facilitator in advance if unable to attend. Three consecutive absences will signify inability to continue serving as a team

member. We agree to abide by quorum decisions made in our absence, and to get needed information from the minutes.

7. *Directness/Support.* If any team member is dissatisfied with the way a meeting is going, he or she will report this directly to the team while it is in session. If a team member tells another member of a dissatisfaction with, or desired change in, some aspect of the team functioning outside of a meeting, the other member will suggest that he or she bring the matter up with the total team at the next meeting. We agree to support and accept each other and to support decisions made by the group. If you think something is good, say it! If you think there is a problem or conflict of interest, please say so.

8. *Debriefing.* We agree to offer everyone an opportunity to debrief before the end of each meeting.

9. *Task List.* At each meeting we will compile a list of tasks that need to be accomplished, the individual(s) who agree to carry out each task, and by when it will be done.

Tool 3. Develop a Common Knowledge Base

What: Developing a common knowledge base is a process for ensuring that all team members have access to necessary information to address the issue with which the team is dealing.

When: Developing a common knowledge base should be done soon after the first team meeting.

Why: A team is more effective when its members start "on the same page" with respect to their knowledge about the issue they plan to address. Developing a common knowledge base based on the education literature provides team members with the "big picture." It also helps the team focus on facts and data, not merely opinions and feelings.

Process for Developing the Knowledge Base

1. Team members brainstorm the common knowledge that they need as a basis for achieving their purpose and summarize ideas on a chart pad.

2. Team members identify possible sources of information or agree to identify sources by the next meeting.

3. Someone on the team gets copies of the key sources to all team members.

4. If there is not too much information, all team members read it before the next meeting. If there is a lot of information, they use the jigsaw method, giving each team member a different section to read and summarize at the next team meeting.

Tool 3

5. In some cases the team may decide it needs to view a video, visit a school site, or obtain information from some other source. If so, volunteers make the necessary arrangements.

Sharing Team Knowledge

A team from Prairieville High School was considering a plan to implement block scheduling. To develop a common knowledge base, they decided they needed information about the advantages and disadvantages of different operational models of block scheduling as reported in the research literature. One team member contacted a regional educational laboratory and was sent 10 articles about block scheduling. Each member took one article to read.

At the next meeting each member reported on his or her article. One person took notes and typed them up, along with the article citations, and sent a copy to each member. When information questions arose in subsequent meetings, the facilitator suggested that the team refer back to its knowledge base.

Tool 4. Clarify Consensus

What: Consensus means that members are sufficiently in favor of a decision that no one will become an obstacle to carrying it out.

When: Clarify consensus when you sense that the team needs to agree on a specific decision or plan of action so that it can move forward.

Why: Team members' support and ownership of ideas is necessary for them to be implemented. Clarifying consensus helps guide team members toward creating that support and ownership.

Operational Definition of Consensus

The following definition is based on the booklet "A Workshop for Convenors" (Eugene Cadre, 1999).

1. All participants contribute, encourage the expression of varied opinions, and view differences as a strength rather than a hindrance.

2. Everyone understands the issue and is able to paraphrase it.

3. Consensus does not mean that the decision gives everyone his or her choice; rather, it means that members sufficiently favor the decision that no one sabotages it or tries to block carrying it out.

4. All share in the final decision; if consensus is not reached, the discussion is automatically recycled to bring more information to bear.

Illustration of Consensus

Consensus is illustrated in figure 1 below. It shows a group of team members (the X's around the outer circle), each of whom holds a somewhat different position from all the other members of the team. Consensus is represented by the smaller circle in the center. Consensus does not represent perfect agreement (the dot in the middle of the smaller circle), but rather a blend of, and reduced range of, perspectives on which all the members are able to reach agreement.

Tool 4

Figure 1

Consensus

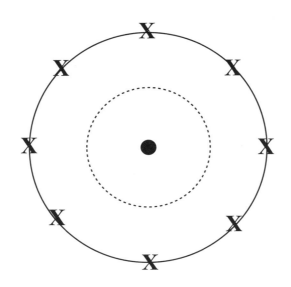

_____ = Original position of each team member (X)

- - - - - - = Consensus

● = Perfect agreement

Guidelines for Moving Toward Consensus

DO present your position logically and provide information to support it.

DO consider other positions carefully before you press your point.

DO acknowledge other positions that have objective and logical bases.

DO explore reasons for differences of opinion.

DO look at alternatives.

DO distinguish between objective data and gut-level feelings about an issue.

DO poll the group often, using **Tool 6,** *Listen for a Breakthrough*, and **Tool 9,** *Ask Yes-No-What Do You Need?*

DO accept "Pass" as a response, but remind members that unless they take a position their views will not be reflected in the team decision.

DON'T argue for your position without any justification.

DON'T argue automatically for your own personal priorities.

DON'T change your mind just to avoid conflict.

DON'T assume that stalemate reflects a win-lose situation.

To emphasize: Consensus does not mean that you get exactly what YOU want. It means that every team member listens to others and tries to formulate a proposal that combines many people's ideas and is agreeable to all.

The Value of Consensus

The following reading, "Benjamin Franklin on Consensus," helps teams grasp the value of seeking consensus.

1. Each team member can read the section individually.

2. Then team members pair up in kaleidoscope groups (see Tool 5) and discuss the reading selection.

3. The team comes back together, and someone from each pair volunteers to summarize their key learnings about consensus.

Benjamin Franklin on Consensus

On September 17, 1787, Benjamin Franklin put in writing his reasons for voting to support the Constitution of the United States, which had been previously drafted. Franklin's statement represents the combination of tolerance and concern for consensus that is the essence of a democratic society and a prime responsibility of educated men and women. His words are worth contemplating today, when many people find themselves in increasing conflict over the nature and meaning of public events and sense a great need for mutual tolerance and humility.

"Mr. President, I confess there are several parts of this Constitution which I do not at present approve, but I am not sure that I shall never approve them: for having lived long, I have experienced many instances of being obliged by better information or fuller consideration to change opinions even on more important subjects, which I once thought right, but found to be otherwise. It is therefore that the older I grow, the more apt I am to doubt my own judgment, and to pay more respect to the judgment of others.

"In these sentiments, Sir, I agree to this Constitution with all its faults, if they are such, because I think a general Government necessary for us and there is no form of Government but what may be a blessing to the people if well administered, and believe further, that this is likely to be well administered for a course of years, and can only end in Despotism, as other forms have done before it, when the people have become so corrupted as to need despotic Government, being incapable of any other. I doubt, too, whether any other Convention we can obtain may be able to make a better Constitution. For when you assemble a number of men to have the advantage of their joint wisdom, you inevitably assemble with those men all their prejudices, their passions, their errors of opinion, their local interests, and their selfishness. From such an assembly can a perfect production be expected? It therefore, astonishes me, Sir, to find this system approaching so near perfection as it does and I think it will astonish our enemies, who are waiting with confidence to hear that our councils are confounded like those of the builders of Babel; and that our States are on the point of separation, only to meet hereafter for the purpose of cutting one another's throats.

"Thus I consent, Sir, to this Constitution because I expect no better, and because I am not sure it is not the best.... On the whole, Sir, I cannot help expressing a wish that every member of the Convention who may still have objections to it, would with me, on this occasion, doubt a little of his own infallibility—and to make manifest our unanimity, put his name to this instrument."

Tool 4

Tool 5. Form Kaleidoscope Groups

What: Kaleidoscope groups are a means to get people with different perspectives together to talk.

When: Kaleidoscope groups should be used when it is important for team members to understand multiple perspectives.

Why: People often get stuck in their own beliefs, seeing situations or proposals only from their own perspectives. They often need help to see the multiple perspectives that may exist about the issue being considered.

Process for Forming Kaleidoscope Groups

1. The metaphor of kaleidoscope groups can be explained like this: "When you look into a kaleidoscope, you see many different pieces of glass of many different colors and shapes. Yet they come together into a beautiful design. In much the same way, when a group of people come together as a work team, each one brings his or her own perspective. However, if each team member can understand and respect multiple perspectives, the team is more likely to be able to bring those perspectives together into a powerful proposal that can be supported by the group—that is, a consensus."

2. In order for the group to begin to understand multiple perspectives, members need to interact with people they don't know well, or who have different jobs and different interests. Ask team members to pair up with someone they don't know well, someone who has a different job, or

someone with different interests related to the issue on which the team plans to work.

3. The members in each small group can take 5 to 10 minutes to discuss their positions on the team issue. Suggest that they look for the similarities in their positions as well as discussing their differences.

4. The small groups should end their discussions in time to do a Round Robin (sometimes called a Power Sweep; see Tool 11). This involves asking, "How does everyone feel about the idea (or topic/issue/goal/proposal) at this point? What else would you like to know about it before you feel ready to work on it?" Give each team member a chance to respond briefly.

Seeking Common Ground

The community of Wicker recently experienced a violent incident in one of its schools. The school superintendent asked a team of community and school representatives to address the issue of how to keep students safe in school. Some team members were known to favor measures aimed at improving security in the schools, such as the use of metal detectors or security guards. Others had expressed concerns about protecting students' rights.

The facilitator asked the team to form kaleidoscope groups that represented both viewpoints. She sensed that discussion between individuals who differed in their perspective would help the team in its efforts to arrive at proposals with a good chance to achieve consensus.

Tool 5

Phase II. Working Toward Consensus

In addition to concentrating talent and energy to address an important issue, a major benefit of a work team is that its membership can reflect the varied perspectives of stakeholders who are concerned about the issue. Ideally, members of the team with which you are working represent the varied constituencies whose needs must be served. The team leader must ensure that members' varied perspectives have a chance to be expressed, shared, and accommodated in order to help the team move toward consensus.

Before introducing nine tools for working toward consensus, we will mention some strategies that have proved helpful to encourage all the members of a work team to contribute to the discussion of issues.

Encouraging Team Discussion of Issues

Sometimes one or more members of a team does not volunteer ideas, chooses to pass when the leader asks for group input, or expresses a noncommittal, "fence-sitting" position when the leader asks for responses to a proposal. Others, by contrast, tend to dominate the discussion, or even attempt to reopen issues that the group has already decided. Some ways to get everyone to speak up are:

Say that attending team meetings is itself a form of participation, and that you appreciate people showing up. Ask people to "share the airspace," meaning that they note how much time is available and how many people need to be heard and take those facts into account in determining how long they speak.

Before recognizing the first person who wants to speak, remind the entire group, "Everyone's views need to be taken into account, so I'd like to hear from each of you."

When you are asking each person to express his or her views on a specific issue give people the chance to pass, but indicate you'll come back to them after others have spoken. Then follow up, asking those who initially passed to express their views.

Phase II. Working Toward Consensus

Explain to a fence-sitter that the team's decision-making process involves a forced choice—for example, either "I like the proposal," "I dislike the proposal," or "I'm not sure yet how I feel about the proposal." Point out that if someone continues to pass it excludes that person from the process, while even saying "I'm not sure yet" helps clarify where the team is and what the leader needs to do to help the team move forward.

Remind members that being on the team involves a commitment to express their opinions, to seek agreement on steps that will allow the team to move forward, and to live with the team's decisions. Also note your commitment, if possible, to making team meetings a safe place for members to "discuss the undiscussables." This means that you encourage members to share their own resistance or fears, and any major anticipated problems that have not surfaced yet. Explain that this does not mean the meetings are open season for criticizing or bitching. Suggest that in speaking people focus on perceived or predicted behavior rather than to make judgments and interpretations about others.

You might want to suggest a standard procedure for obtaining input from team members who were absent from a specific meeting. Alternately, you can ask the team for suggestions, or for volunteers to obtain input from absentees.

The question might arise as to whether someone can both serve as the team leader and participate in group activities and decisions along with other team members. We recommend that the team first check its group agreements, to see whether they specify who are voting members. If the leader is a voting member, he or she should be free to participate.

It is often difficult, however, to lead a meeting and participate fully at the same time, particularly when high-stakes issues are on the table. In that case, the team might wish to introduce a different procedure for leading the meeting. Some possibilities are to:

- bring in an outside facilitator to lead a particular team activity.
- rotate leadership among team members, so that a different member serves as the leader for each meeting.
- have the leader turn the leadership function over to someone else while he or she takes a turn, if a vote, opinion, or other group activity is called for.

• switch team leaders at specific intervals during the meeting, say every 20 minutes.

Here we describe nine tools for helping a team share the perspectives of different team members so that it can consider appropriate solutions to the problem it is addressing and work toward consensus on those solutions. In the process, team members develop a realistic sense of the team's talent base, as well as its level of commitment and energy for implementing the solutions that are endorsed.

Tool 6, *Fly the Helicopter Higher* helps the team focus on big ideas about which consensus is possible rather than on small and potentially divisive details.

• **Tool 7,** *Float a Trial Balloon* allows team members to share the positives of a proposal before sharing areas of concern.

• **Tool 8,** *Ask Yes-No-What Do You Need?* helps clarify the extent of member agreement with a proposal and the conditions that a modified proposal must include to satisfy various members of the team.

• **Tool 9,** *Brainstorm From* → *To* focuses on the inevitability of change and helps mobilize the team to propose actions that will move it toward its vision.

• **Tool 10,** *Listen for a Breakthrough* shows team members how to listen and respond to each other's ideas in ways that promote the emergence of creative and mutually satisfying proposals.

• **Tool 11,** *Call for a Power Sweep* encourages each team member to express his or her feelings about the idea that the team is considering.

- **Tool 12,** *Do a Five-Finger Share* allows team members to express the precise level of their agreement or disagreement with a proposal.

- **Tool 13,** *Take a Backup Vote* enables a quorum of team members to express support for a proposal so that it can be implemented even though consensus has not been reached.

- **Tool 14,** *Test for Critical Mass* allows the team leader to determine when there is sufficient support for a proposal to implement it even though consensus has not been reached.

Tool 6. Fly the Helicopter Higher: Focus on Big Ideas

What: *Fly the Helicopter Higher* is a process for helping team members focus on big ideas rather than on specific details when considering proposals for action.

When: Use *Fly the Helicopter Higher* when you sense team members are focusing on specific details surrounding an issue and losing sight of their common purpose as a result.

Why: Teams often disagree or fall apart because they get hung up on specific details rather than attending to the big ideas that serve their purpose and how to realize those ideas. *Fly the Helicopter Higher* helps team members refocus on big ideas.

The Process of Flying the Helicopter Higher

1. The facilitator should note points during the discussion of a proposal when one or more members appear to be focusing on, or arguing about, very specific details.

2. Point out that team agreement on such fine details is unlikely, because of the diversity of viewpoints that the team represents.

3. Ask the team to "fly the helicopter a little higher," that is, to focus on the big ideas.

Focusing on Big Ideas Leads to Consensus

The Prairieville High School team, while considering a proposal to initiate a block schedule at the school, was arguing about how long each period should be: 90 minutes, 100 minutes, or somewhere in between.

The team leader asked the team to "fly their helicopter higher" by focussing on the purpose of block scheduling. She reminded the team that the purpose of the block-schedule proposal was to provide enough time for hands-on, relevant instruction for all students. Several team members then became willing to compromise and pick a period length that seemed reasonable so that they could move forward.

Tool 7. Float a Trial Balloon

What: Floating a trial balloon is used to ensure that team members will respond with positive comments when a new idea is introduced.

When: A trial balloon is used when a new idea is introduced and you want the team to focus on the positives of the idea before considering the negatives.

Why: Some people greet almost any new idea with negative comments, which represents the "shoot-it-down" syndrome. Team members may stop bringing up new ideas because of their fear of having them shot down. Floating a trial balloon blocks the shoot-it-down syndrome.

The Process of Floating a Trial Balloon

1. When a team member has a new idea to propose, he or she introduces it to the team.

2. For ten minutes, only positive comments about the idea are accepted and recorded on a chart pad. If anyone starts to raise questions or express concerns that reflect negatively on the proposal, remind the team that only positive comments are appropriate now, and that they will have an opportunity to ask clarifying questions or express concerns later.

3. After ten minutes, the team gets equal time to ask clarifying questions or to express concerns.

4. Ask everyone to listen to all the comments to see if there is a way to state the proposal in a form that will get them to consensus. Remind team members to "shorten the runway" (see Top Tip #12) when it is their turn so that there is time to hear from everyone.

5. When everyone has shared their ideas, ask if any of the team members can generate a proposal that may get them to consensus, or generate a proposal yourself.

6. Use Tool 11 to call for a power sweep before ending the meeting. This involves going around the room again so that each team member can say how he or she feels about the proposal at this point.

Emphasizing the Positive

A subcommittee of Genuine Middle School presented a proposal at a meeting of all teachers to create a school-within-a-school that would specialize in helping at-risk students. During the *Float a Trial Balloon* process, teachers made a variety of positive comments about the proposal, including:

- **"Because this school will focus on students at risk, class size will be lower."**

- **"The students will still get a regular reading-language arts-social studies block, but with lower student enrollment."**

- **"I like that the students will have positive role models."**

- **"Teachers who like working with at-risk students will have more chances to provide service."**

- **"It's an innovative way to support at-risk students in a time of diminishing resources."**

Tool 8. Ask Yes-No-What Do You Need?

What: To help a team move toward consensus, this process clarifies which team members support a proposal and what team members who do not support the proposal would need in order to support it (or an alternate proposal to which all can agree).

When: Use *Ask Yes-No-What Do You Need?* when you sense that the team is approaching consensus on a particular proposal and you want to clarify what team members who are not in support would need in order to support it.

Why: To reach consensus, team members who do not support a proposal must be given the opportunity to state what they would need in order to support it. The information they provide is then used by all team members to modify the proposal in such a way that everyone can accept it (that is, reach consensus).

The Ask Yes-No-What Do You Need? Process

1. Someone states the proposal and it is written on a chart pad.

2. Each member states either:

    a. Yes, I support the proposal, and (if he or she wishes) why, **OR**

    b. No, I don't support the proposal, and this is what I would need in order to support it.

3. The Yes/No responses are tallied on a chart (see the example that follows), with a summary of what people responding No would need in order to support the proposal. If people responding Yes also express

needs, record their responses as Yes but also record what they say they need.

4. This process does not constitute a vote for or against the proposal. It is simply a means of collecting information on how the team feels about the proposal at this point. When the chart is filled in, all team members look at the data in the "I need" row and think of how the original proposal could be modified in a way that will help the team move toward consensus.

5. If the team still cannot reach consensus after trying multiple proposals, the facilitator could try using **Tool 13,** *Take a Backup Vote*, or **Tool 14,** *Test for Critical Mass.*

Clarifying Team Members' Needs

Masterful Middle School's eight teachers met in June to consider a proposal from three of the teachers: To schedule a week-long orientation and study-skills workshop for all fifth-graders during the week before classes begin this fall. The other five teachers' responses were recorded:

Team Members	YES	NO	I NEED
Jim	X		To work with the special ed teacher to teach reading skills.
Phil	X		
Linda		X	To know how many hours this will add to my teaching load.
Kathryn		X	An estimate of the cost and where the funds will come from.
Eric	X		To know what the projected enrollment for fall will be to help me in putting together a schedule.

Ask Yes-No-What Do You Need?

After reviewing the teachers' comments for a moment, the facilitator summed up the results this way: "Altogether, six teachers support the proposal—the three who stated it and the other three who said Yes. The two teachers who said No need information on the time demands and the financial impact of the proposal, both for the school and for them personally. A couple of the team members who said Yes need to know more about the teaching load and about whether they can work with other teachers in teaching the orientation classes." The facilitator also noted that the team would take steps to get the needs met of both the members who said Yes and those who said No.

Tool 9. Brainstorm From → To

What: *Brainstorm From → To* allows team members to compare the past and future with respect to a particular phenomenon.

When: Use the *Brainstorm From → To* process when you want team members to reflect on and discuss how a particular phenomenon has changed over time.

Why: Brainstorming future scenarios helps team members envision the future and create desired changes, and reflecting on how much change has already occurred helps them stay open to moving forward.

The Brainstorm From → To Process

1. For teams with more than six members, divide the team into two or more smaller groups.

2. Each group draws a line down the middle of a piece of chart-pad paper and labels the left side FROM and the right side TO.

3. Each group reflects on a particular phenomenon. You can assign topics or let groups pick their topics. A humorous example about life for baby boomers (that is, people born in the U.S. between 1946 and 1950) and an example concerning parent-school communication follow.

4. Each group summarizes on its sheet the changes that have occurred in the phenomenon it is considering by recording specific examples of what the phenomenon was like at some point in the past (FROM) and what it is like today or what they want it to become in the future (TO).

Life for Baby Boomers

FROM	→	TO
Long hair	→	Longing for hair
Acid rock	→	Acid reflux
Keg	→	EKG
Growing pot	→	Growing a pot
Seeds and stems	→	Roughage
Hoping for a BMW	→	Hoping for a BM
Our president's struggle with Fidel	→	Our president's struggle with fidelity
Getting out to a new, hip joint	→	Getting a new hip joint

Parent-School Communication at Hallelujah School

FROM	→	TO
Teachers assume that parents are supporting students' learning at home.	→	Teachers request parent signoff on assignments, and provide parent contracts/written guidelines/classes.
Written communications for parents are sent home with students.	→	Parents get a parent newsletter each month and occasional school communications by phone, e-mail, or mail.
Parent-teacher conferences occur in person, at school, during school hours.	→	Parent-teacher conferences occur at mutually convenient times and locations, using the communication mode that works best.
Parents learn of their children's problems or successes from the students' report cards.	→	Teachers give every parent regular progress reports about each of their children.
Parents are not informed of the most effective ways to communicate with school personnel.	→	Parents get an updated list of the room, phone number, and e-mail address of all their children's teachers and other key school personnel and best times to reach them.

Tool 10. Listen for a Breakthrough

What: *Listen for a Breakthrough* is a process that encourages members to listen to one another's ideas with respect, empathy, and openness, continuing to modify a proposal until all members' key needs are met.

When: Sometimes teams have difficulty identifying all the needs of members who vote No during the use of **Tool 8,** *Ask Yes-No-What Do You Need?* If that occurs, use *Listen for a Breakthrough,* which encourages all team members to help the members voting NO clarify what they would need in order to get to Yes.

Why: For team members to work well together and make appropriate proposals, they must listen respectfully to each other's ideas and consider a whole range of ways of dealing with issues.

Process of Listening for a Breakthrough

1. Explain that to reach consensus, each team member must be willing to move from his or her position toward the position of members with different perspectives. The breakthrough for which they must listen is a way to modify the proposal so that the team can reach consensus.

2. After one team member has expressed his or her perspective, do a listening check, perhaps by engaging in the following exercise: "Everyone take out a sheet of paper and write down what Joe just said." Have team

members compare what they wrote, and note who paraphrased Joe's statement most accurately.

3. Explain that the kind of listening required for an effective work team involves more than being able to paraphrase what others say, though that is important. Team members also must listen with *empathy,* which means putting yourself mentally and emotionally in someone else's place so completely that you know what it feels like to walk in the other person's shoes.

4. The idea of moving toward other members' perspectives is illustrated in figure 2 (page 42). It is the same as the consensus circle (figure 1) in **Tool 4,** *Clarify Consensus*, except that figure 2 shows each team member (the X's around the outer circle) moving closer to other members' perspectives (the arrows pointing inward). The process of moving closer is accomplished by looking for common themes and seeking a blend, or reduced range, of perspectives on which all the members can reach consensus.

5. Remind the team that the "breakthrough" for which they must listen is how to modify a proposal to take into account the needs of all members. Also point out the principal of synergy, or 1 + 1 = 3, meaning that a proposal that builds on the ideas of all team members is usually superior to a proposal suggested by one member, because all members enrich it.

6. Team members respond to each suggested proposal modification either with Yes or No. If a member's position is still No, the member should identify what he or she would need to move to Yes.

7. Continue this process until the team appears ready to accept by consensus the latest modification of the proposal. If consensus still is not reached, you might want to try **Tool 13,** *Take a Backup Vote*, giving any remaining members still at No a chance to stand aside so that the team can move forward.

8. Sometimes this process takes the team in a different direction from the one in which it was heading before. The breakthrough might be a very different proposal from what most of the team members were favoring previously, but one that they can all support. For example, a high school teacher who taught creative writing was struggling with the issue of how to get students to do more writing in order to increase their writing skills. Most teachers' ideas for dealing with this concern are fairly traditional, like giving students more written assignments or asking parents to help their children write letters. The creative writing teacher came up with a breakthrough idea. He told his students that for the next 18 weeks he would not speak in class, but would deliver all his communications in written form. The teacher reported that "Each day in class brought greater student input . . . . If I was talking less and writing more, they could talk less and write more" (Ryan, 1991).

Tool 10

Figure 2

Moving Toward Consensus

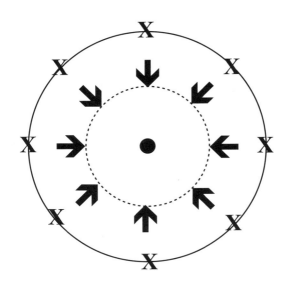

_____	=	Original position of each team member (X)
➔	=	Moving closer to other members' perspectives
- - - - -	=	Consensus
●	=	Perfect agreement

Working for a Breakthrough

A Merrydale High School student team was planning a raffle to raise money for sports equipment. The team members and other students planned to donate items to create a pool of raffle prizes. Janet proposed that in the raffle the student holding the first winning ticket could pick any item in the pool, the student holding the next winning ticket could take any remaining item, and so forth until all the items were taken.

Mark said that he had an exercise bike he could donate. Because the bike's value was far greater than that of the other items likely to be donated, Mark suggested a separate raffle for the bike, with more expensive raffle tickets. Janet disagreed, saying she thought they should keep the raffle simple, with whoever held the first winning ticket being able to pick either the bike or any other item.

At this point the team took a backup vote. All the other team members said that they preferred having a single raffle in order to keep things simple. The team leader asked if they could modify their proposal to take Mark's need into account. After some thought, Janet proposed that anyone who wanted to win the exercise bike would have to buy at least five raffle tickets in order to qualify for that prize. Mark found this plan acceptable, so the team found its breakthrough and reached consensus.

Tool 10

Tool 11. Call for a Power Sweep

What: *Call for a Power Sweep* involves asking every team member to take a turn expressing his or her feelings about the idea or proposal that the team is considering.

When: Use *Call for a Power Sweep* when a proposal has been generated and you want the team to listen to each member's feelings and ideas about the proposal.

Why: Getting everyone's input provides synergy (see Top Tip #2). By moving the proposal beyond one person to a concept in which all the members share, the team can see that the whole is greater than the sum of its parts: $1 + 1 = 3$. This increases the opportunity for the team to reach consensus.

The Process of Calling for a Power Sweep

1. State that it is now a good time for all team members to share their ideas and feelings about the idea or proposal in order to help the team move toward consensus.
2. Go around the room and invite each member to share, asking them to keep their comments brief and on the topic.

Sensing the Power of a Power Sweep

A teacher team from Aspen Elementary School developed a proposal for a foundation grant to support a family resource center at the school. Now

Tool 11

they want to present the proposal to the school site council for approval to send it to the foundation.

At the site council meeting, the team leader gives a written summary of the proposal to each member and gives them a few minutes to read it. Then she suggests that they go around the room to hear everyone's reactions to the proposal. With her encouragement, the parent member, who is usually quiet, speaks up with enthusiasm in support of the family resource center idea. Other site council members agree, and then suggest some minor changes to the wording of the summary. The team leader thanks them for their time, and leaves the meeting confident that she has obtained the site council's support for establishing a resource center.

Tool 11

Tool 12. Do a Five-Finger Share

What: *Five-Finger Share* lets each team member show how he or she feels about a proposal by holding up one to five fingers.

When: Use *Five-Finger Share* to see if the team is at or near consensus, which represents all members voting 3, 4, or 5 on the proposal.

Why: A *Five-Finger Share* allows the team to quickly sense the level of support for a proposal.

What each number represents:

Five fingers: Love—I support the idea and will work actively to help it become a reality.

Four fingers: Really like—I support the idea; while I may not be a major player, I will do what is appropriate.

Three fingers: Neutral—I'm not opposed to the idea; I don't care if others want to do it; I won't undermine their efforts.

Two fingers: Really dislike—I prefer other options. While I dislike the proposal, I will abide by the decision of the group for at least a trial period of time and I will not "sabotage" the decision.

One finger: Hate—I am opposed to the idea.

The Five-Finger Share process:

1.   Figure 3 on page 49 is a more detailed version of figure 1 from **Tool 4,** *Clarify Consensus*. It represents an agreement target, which is similar in design to a dart board. The outermost circle (1) represents one finger; the next circle in (2) represents two fingers; and the next three circles in all

represent consensus, that is, sufficient team agreement to move the proposal forward, with the third circle in (3) representing three fingers, the fourth circle in representing four fingers , and the fifth circle in representing five fingers. Note that three fingers corresponds to the line representing consensus in figure 1, while five fingers corresponds to the point representing perfect agreement in figure 1. Reproduce the target on the board or a chart pad before stating the proposal to be considered, and make a mark on the target for each team member's position.

2. Each team member raises one to five fingers to indicate how he or she feels about the proposal.

3. If everyone in the group raises three, four, or five fingers, consensus has been reached.

4. If any team members raise just one or two fingers, each of them states what they would need before they could raise three, four, or five fingers.

5. If some team members raise one or two fingers, try **Tool 10**, *Listen for a Breakthrough*, to help the team reach consensus.

6. Sometimes a team cannot reach consensus after trying multiple proposals. In that case, use **Tool 13,** *Take a Backup Vote*, or **Tool 14,** *Test for Critical Mass*, to determine whether there is sufficient agreement to move forward.

7. If consensus still is not reached, the leader can ask members who still are at one or two fingers if they are willing to stand aside, which they can indicate by holding one finger sideways rather than pointed up. By standing aside, a member declares willingness not to block the proposal from being accepted in order to allow the team to move forward.

Tool 12

Figure 3

Agreement Target

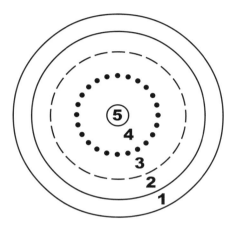

Assessing Each Member's Level of Agreement

Last year Courtland College began offering an introductory genetics course on the World Wide Web. Some 250 students worldwide took the course, participating in on-line discussions with other students and the five course consultants at Courtland.

Now the consultants want to evaluate the course design, with an eye to expanding it to other courses. Tori, one of the course consultants, has proposed that they post the evaluation on the Web and ask students about any minuses they see to taking courses in electronic form. She also volunteered to draft a questionnaire if the consultant team accepts her proposal.

Tool 12

The head consultant felt that the group could reach consensus quickly, but wanted to give everyone a chance to express their position in the shortest time possible. So he drew an agreement target on the board and asked for a five-finger share. All five consultants raised either three, four, or five fingers, so Tori promised to have a draft of the questionnaire ready in one week.

Determining the Extent of Agreement

At a recent meeting of the board for the family resource center housed at Wilson Elementary School, board members were asked to express agreement or disagreement with a grant proposal to be submitted to a foundation.

One team member, Susan, thought that the purpose to which the funds were to be put was not consistent with the foundation's guidelines, so she objected to the proposal. After some discussion the team leader called for a five-finger share. Each team member, including Susan, raised three, four, or five fingers, so the team leader declared that consensus had now been reached.

Tool 13. Take a Backup Vote

What: A backup vote is a vote to determine whether a proposal has enough support to move forward.

When: A backup vote is used when the team has not reached consensus. It is more precise than using **Tool 14,** *Test for Critical Mass.*

Why: Taking a backup vote provides a way for the team to move forward by revealing whether the majority of team members support the proposal.

The Backup Vote Process

1. A team member needs to clearly state the proposal; it is helpful to write it on a chart pad as well.

2. Other team members may ask only clarifying questions concerning the proposal. This is not the time to reopen a debate or make statements as to why the proposal might not work.

3. Generally a quorum is necessary to take a backup vote. A quorum means that a majority of team members (that is, one more than half) must be present. If a quorum is not present, you will probably have to table the proposal until the next meeting.

4. Each team member votes either to support or reject the proposal. If a majority of those present (that is, one more than half) accept the proposal, the backup vote is positive and the team can move forward on the proposal.

5. Ask each of the members who voted to reject the proposal if they want to stand aside. This means that, while they are still not in favor of the proposal, they agree not to block it from being accepted and to allow the team to move forward.

6. What happens if you suspect that some team members might miss a meeting to prevent the team from having a quorum?

    a. Arrange the time and location of team meetings to suit as many team members' schedules as possible, and announce future meetings well in advance.

    b. Make clear that group agreements specify that all team members agree to attend each meeting.

    c. Track who is not at the meeting, and talk to absent members about their nonattendance before the next meeting.

    d. Assume that people rarely miss meetings intentionally, but that circumstances sometimes prevent individuals from attending meetings.

Taking a Backup Vote to Promote Forward Movement

The Emerald City High School site council spent several months gathering information from school and community stakeholders on the perceived pros and cons of block scheduling. At the next staff meeting they sought staff consensus on a plan to implement block scheduling in the fall.

Several members of the site council tried stating a proposal for the block schedule plan. After discussion the team leader, Joe, asked staff members to express their level of agreement with each proposal. Each attempt to reach consensus was unsuccessful, with one or more members expressing disagreement.

After counting noses, Joe saw that more than half of the staff were still at the meeting, though several looked as though they were about to leave. At that point Joe called for a backup vote on the last proposal they had heard. A majority of those present voted to support the proposal. Joe called the meeting to a close, noting that the site council could now move forward on that proposal. "So we'll develop a plan for the fall, and as we do we'll address the concerns that you still have," Joe concluded.

Waiting for a Quorum

A work team was scheduled to present its draft of a questionnaire to survey all Bowling Green Middle School teachers about their views of block scheduling. At the teachers meeting a draft of the questionnaire was presented, but several team members who had helped design it were absent.

The presenter explained that the superintendent had asked the team to make a report about the planned survey at the school board meeting that evening, and team members were busy preparing their report. The team leader pointed out that the survey might be modified anyway after the board meeting, and suggested that the teachers delay voting on the proposal until its next teacher meeting.

Tool 14. Test for Critical Mass

What: Critical mass is the approximate number of team members who must support a proposal for it to be implemented. Not a precise number, it represents the facilitator's sense that there is enough support for the proposal to make it likely to succeed.

When: Test for critical mass when the team has not reached consensus but you sense that there might be sufficient support for a proposal to implement it.

Why: Implementation of new ideas is often difficult. You need to determine if there are enough "cheerleaders" behind an idea to make it go. They represent critical mass.

Guidelines for Determining the Number of Team Members Needed for Critical Mass

1. It is up to the facilitator to sense when the number of team members in support of a proposal indicates critical mass. This judgment is not precise but only approximate, and depends on the team "feel."

2. Generally, the smaller the total number of team members, the higher the number (that is, the proportion of members) necessary for critical mass. Conversely, the larger the total number of team members, the lower the number (that is, the proportion of members) necessary for critical mass.

3. In some situations, critical mass depends on not only the number of team members who are in support of a proposal, but also the particular members who support it. For example, some members may be key stakehold-

Tool 14

ers with respect to a particular proposal, while acceptance of the proposal will have less impact on other members who are not key stakeholders. In this case, you might sense that critical mass was not present unless at least a majority of members from the key-stakeholder group support the proposal.

Sensing Critical Mass

At Graves Elementary School four educational assistants supervise playground activities and attend faculty meetings with the school's eight teachers, but do not participate in implementing curriculum decisions. At its next faculty meeting, which you will facilitate, the team will consider a proposal to adopt the Finesse Reading Series texts for students in grades 1 through 3.

Imagine that all but one of the teachers were to agree with the proposal but two educational assistants did not. In that case you probably would assume critical mass, because the teachers are the team members who will use the textbook series.

On the other hand, imagine that all the educational assistants were enthusiastic about the reading series but only one or two teachers supported it. You would probably not consider this level of support to represent critical mass.

Phase III. Moving into Action

Nearly every work team has some form of action as its ultimate purpose. For example, many specific actions are required of teams whose purpose is to align a school curriculum with state standards, and to determine needs for teacher inservice for teaching the modified curriculum. All the tools we have described thus far will help a team develop the best possible proposals and plans for action as it carries out its work.

In this final section, we describe three tools that are particularly important in helping a team achieve the broad goals for which it was created or convened.

- **Tool 15,** *Cluster Idea Cards* helps team members quickly generate and synthesize a large number of ideas bearing on the issue that the team needs to address.

- **Tool 16,** *Spend Your Dots* provides two approaches to help members set priorities on the ideas for action that emerge from their list of ideas.

- **Tool 17,** *Develop an Action Timeline* helps the team prioritize and set timelines for completing actions that will be carried out.

Tool 15. Cluster Idea Cards

What: Clustering idea cards allows a team to organize a large number of ideas concerning an issue.

When: Have the team write and cluster idea cards whenever it needs to pull together a lot of information and ideas to help clarify its future direction.

Why: There are times when large amounts of information need to be synthesized for the team's review as a guide to moving forward.

The Process of Clustering Idea Cards

1. Using 3" x 5" note cards (or post-it notes), team members list ideas concerning the issue being considered, writing each idea on a separate card, front side only. So that the cards can be easily read, ask members to state each idea briefly and print it in large, dark print.

2. If the team has more than six members, break it into two or more groups. Each group takes a stack of idea cards and clusters them by putting together the ideas that have something in common.

3. Team members give each cluster of idea cards a name representing the big concept of what all the ideas in that cluster have in common, and write the name for each cluster on a separate card. For example, a team might be considering a proposal to extend the school year for two weeks. It might find that some ideas have to do with fears about the effects on

parents, and other ideas are related to concerns about financing a longer school year.

4. The members of each group take a final look at the cards in each cluster to see if any clusters should be combined or renamed, if any cards should be moved, or if any new clusters are needed.

5. To help the team focus on the ideas most relevant to its purpose, you might first want to review **Tool 1,** *State a Purpose*. It might also help to first review **Tool 6,** *Fly the Helicopter Higher*, to remind team members to focus on big ideas.

Identifying Ideas

A team of Head Start teachers in the community of Greenborough was considering a proposal to reduce its schedule of parent classes during the summer because of poor attendance at some classes held the previous summer. When they wrote idea cards and clustered them, one cluster had to do with fears about the effects on parents in need, and another cluster involved concerns about teachers losing salary or being laid off if classes were reduced.

Tool 16. Spend Your Dots

What: *Spend Your Dots* allows a team to prioritize ideas for action by revealing members' level of support for various idea clusters.

When: When it is important to determine the team's top priorities, have the team spend its dots using equal distribution. When it is important for each team member to be able to express the intensity of his or her preferences, have the team spend its dots using weighted distribution.

Why: For the team to reach consensus, you need to help members set priorities. This process allows the team to set priorities in a fair and nonthreatening manner.

The Spend-Your-Dots Process

1. Depending on the number of idea card clusters that need to be prioritized, each team member receives the same number of self-stick dots (or post-it notes).

2. Team members use their dots to prioritize.

   a. For equal distribution, each member puts each of his or her dots on the name card for a different cluster of idea cards. A member can put only one dot on each name card.

   b. For weighted distribution, each member puts each of his or her dots on the name card for one *or more* specific clusters of idea cards. A member can put anywhere from one to the total number of dots on a particular name card.

3. After all dots have been applied, the name cards with the most dots are the top-priority items.

Prioritizing Needs

At a special board session of the Wilson Elementary School family resource center, board members distributed their dots among nine idea card clusters. Three clusters received the largest number of dots: (1) simplifying the organizational structure of the center, (2) reviewing the programs provided to families that use the center, and (3) clarifying the board's role in decision-making versus policy-setting. A subcommittee then met to develop action proposals to address these issues.

Tool 17. Develop an Action Timeline

What: *Develop an Action Timeline* involves putting the actions that the team identifies as high priority in the order of what needs to happen first, second, third, and so forth. After team members agree on the sequence of actions, they also specify (for example, by month) when they want each action to be completed.

When: Use *Develop an Action Timeline* when the team is ready to develop a long-term plan of action.

Why: People need a place to begin. This process allows the team to break its planned tasks into small parts so that it can get started.

The Process of Developing an Action Timeline

1. After the team has completed categorizing, naming, and prioritizing each group of idea cards (see Tools 15 and 16), ask the team to put the name cards for each group of cards that involve high-priority actions in order of what needs to happen first, second, third, and so forth.

2. Once they have put all the name cards in order, ask members to indicate for each card when they want each action completed. See the example that follows of a school's action timeline for developing a school improvement plan.

3. Once the name cards have been ordered and dated, have the timeline typed up so that it can serve as a step-by-step guide for, and provide benchmarks toward, achieving tasks.

Action Timeline

> # Before or by the specified date, the School Improvement Team for Bandana Middle School will take the following actions:
>
> | September 30 | October 15 | October 31 | November 30 |
> | --- | --- | --- | --- |
> | Explain to team members the duties of site councils. | Elect site council members and make group agreements. | Look at student profile data.

Determine strengths and areas needing continuous improvement. | Develop draft of school-improvement plan.

Present plan to whole staff.

Assign subcommittee for each major task.

Present plan to school board. |

Tool **17**

Preparing Other Team Leaders

Now that we have presented all seventeen of the tools in this Toolkit, we will share some ideas for using the tools to prepare other team leaders.

The Toolkit can be used to prepare team members to assume leadership. In this age of shared decision-making, all team members are responsible for moving the team forward. Therefore, it is important that every member feels comfortable to provide leadership, or share the facilitator role when necessary. The Toolkit also can be used to prepare team members for leadership in other task forces or work teams on which they will serve.

You can point out natural opportunities for leadership within the team, or design team activities to help other members share the leadership role. You might suggest possible tasks for which they can volunteer, such as summarizing key points of the discussion on a chart pad, adding suggested items to the agenda, or rephrasing unclear points brought up by one member to help other members understand them.

We suggest that you carry out the following coaching activities to help team members develop skills in selecting and applying tools to facilitate teamwork. As members make comments, use the tool cards and your own experience to coach them toward proficiency in use of the tools.

Coaching Activities

1. Ask team members to pair up. Each pair identifies a real-life team or group situation where something is not going well, or it is difficult to reach consensus. They choose a tool that they feel would improve the situation. Have each pair describe the situation, how they would use that tool to address it, and what they hope to accomplish by using that tool.

2. Unlike Activity 1, in which team members can pick any tool they like, this activity requires them to identify real-life situations where each of the tools would be useful. Team members pair up, and each pair picks (or you can assign them) a particular tool. The pair identifies a real-life team or group situation where that tool would be useful. They describe the situation, how they would use that tool to address it, and what they hope to accomplish.

3. To model use of the tools, provide brief real-life examples of how you have used or could use particular tools to lead a team in deciding a specific issue. For example, a district curriculum coordinator described her use of the following tools to facilitate a teacher team considering block scheduling for the district's high schools:

   a. **Tool 1,** *State a Purpose.* After brief discussion the team agreed that its purpose was "to determine if there is enough agreement among the high school teaching staff to go to a block schedule."

   b. **Tool 2,** *Set Group Agreements.* By collective consensus the team reached these group agreements: any comment is appropriate as long as it is communicated respectfully; debate issues, not people; no side talking; and be honest.

   c. **Tool 3,** *Develop a Common Knowledge Base.* To develop common knowledge the team completed a jigsaw activity in which they learned about the advantages of using longer blocks of time for instruction.

   d. **Tool 4,** *Clarify Consensus.* The team reflected on the desirability of getting all the high school teachers to agree to block scheduling, or at least agree not to oppose it, before implementation of the proposal.

   e. **Tool 6,** *Fly the Helicopter Higher: Focus on Big Ideas.* Members stated in turn the pros and cons they saw in going to a longer block of time. They did not discuss the specific schedule to be implemented but just talked about the broad concept.

   f. **Tool 7,** *Float a Trial Balloon.* Members were asked in turn to mention positives of using longer blocks of time for instruction, while members with no positives to share could pass.

   g. **Tool 8,** *Ask Yes-No-What Do You Need?* The leader restated the block scheduling proposal, and most team members responded Yes. One team member responding No indicated that before agreeing to the proposal she would need to know that she would still have a planning period early in the school day.

h.   **Tool 10,** *Listen for a Breakthrough.* After listening to the original proposal, some members suggested solutions that addressed others' concerns about time scheduling and moved the team toward consensus.

Quiz on Best Tool to Use

Give team members the following quiz to help them learn the purpose and appropriate use of each tool. Ask them to give the number and name of the best tool to use in each of the following situations. You may wish to form small groups and conduct a competitive activity, in which you read each item and the first group to give the answer is the winner for that item.

1.   A group of educators is holding its first meeting, and the members want to clarify the reason why they will be meeting . Answer: **Tool 1,** *State a Purpose.*

2.   People are getting bogged down in details and have not yet stated a conceptual proposal; you suggest they do this in order to get out of the bog. Answer: **Tool 6,** *Fly the Helicopter Higher.*

3.   Action ideas have been clustered and labeled; now the team needs to decide when they are going to accomplish each action. Answer: **Tool 17,** *Develop an Action Timeline.*

4.   Team members are ready to share their individual, diverse perspectives about the issue. You want the others to hear what each member has to say before they attempt to generate a proposal that is likely to reach consensus. Answer: **Tool 10,** *Listen for a Breakthrough.*

5.   The team wants to determine the changes that need to be made to the proposal on the floor in order to reach critical mass. Answer: **Tool 8,** *Ask Yes-No-What Do You Need?*

6. The group wants to review research about the effectiveness of the program that is being considered for adoption. Answer: **Tool 3,** *Develop a Common Knowledge Base.*

7. The team leader wants the team first to explore the positive aspects of the proposal and hold off on expressing their concerns. Answer: **Tool 7,** *Float a Trial Balloon.*

8. The team is ready to prioritize its ideas for actions to be taken to implement the proposal. Answer: **Tool 16,** *Spend Your Dots.*

9. The team leader wants to encourage members with very different points of view about the issue to get to know each other. Answer: **Tool 5,** *Form Kaleidoscope Groups.*

10. The team needs to synthesize many pieces of information that members have generated in order to clarify its future direction. Answer: **Tool 15,** *Cluster Idea Cards.*

11. The team has not been able to reach consensus, and the leader wants to see how many of the members could support the proposal being considered. Answer: **Tool 13,** *Take a Backup Vote.*

12. The team leader wants to create a safe atmosphere in which all participants feel free to express themselves. Answer: **Tool 2,** *Set Group Agreements.*

13. This process enables the team to see precisely how near they are to consensus. Answer: **Tool 12,** *Do a Five-Finger Share.*

14. This process helps team members discuss how a particular phenomenon they are studying has changed over time. Answer: **Tool 9,** *Brainstorm From → To.*

15. Despite some remaining disagreement, the team leader senses that there is enough overall support to implement the proposal. Answer: **Tool 14,** *Test for Critical Mass.*

16. One member says that she feels that before the group can move forward everyone needs to come to an understanding of the importance of their

being willing to live with whatever decision is reached. Answer: **Tool 4,** *Clarify Consensus.*

Answers (Item Number followed by Tool Number):
1/1; 2/6; 3/17; 4/10; 5/8; 6/3; 7/7; 8/16; 9/5; 10/15; 11/13; 12/2; 13/12; 14/9; 15/14; 16/4.

Top Tips

Leaders need to draw on a wide variety of strategies when unique problems arise in a work team. In addition to the tools already mentioned, many other "top tips" can help make teamwork more pleasant and productive. We encourage you to build these and other ideas into your own unique tools by adapting and expanding on the format provided. To guide you in using these tips, we provide ideas for using one of them—Silos. Also check the recommended readings, which provide many additional ideas for facilitating team meetings and other related topics.

Here we list the top tips to help you find the ones that interest you.

1. **Silos.** The concept of silos illustrates the difference between individuals who view their jobs as separate from the larger system in which they work and those who seek to understand and contribute to that system as a whole. A silo is a large, tall cylinder in which farmers store feed for

livestock. The structure and controlled conditions of silos enable farmers to regulate fermentation and moisture, and minimize spoiling until the feed is needed.

- To help a work team grasp the concept of the silo, you could begin by drawing the analogy between these tall structures, standing in fields and separated by wide open spaces, and how some educators or social-service workers think about their jobs. Like silos, they focus only on their particular job or work setting and spend very little energy thinking about or working to improve the larger environment. Therefore, they have a limited perspective on addressing issues that affect the whole system.

- As an example, imagine that Marzipan School District needs to decide how much staffing each school will get next year. Some building administrators might look at the issue solely in terms of the needs at their school level. You could remind team members to look at the issue from all points of view: "Team members who avoid being silos and look at issues in a holistic fashion increase their usefulness, and indeed their job mobility, to the whole system."

- Activities that could help team members apply the silo concept include: (a) asking them to describe the signs that reveal whether someone is operating in "silo" mode versus remaining open to and connected with the larger environment; (b) asking them to think of colleagues they know who resemble silos, with examples of how those people acted or reacted when particular issues arose; and (c) having team members discuss how they could address the issues facing the team without thinking like silos. For example, an elementary school principal might consider the issue of district staffing not solely in terms of her school's needs, but instead think in terms of how to meet the learning needs of all the students in the district. As facilitator, you might say, "In thinking about the problem, imagine that next year you could be assigned as principal to any other school in the district."

2. **Synergy**. Synergy is the principle that the whole is greater than the sum of its parts, which can also be expressed as "1 + 1 = 3." It is focused on

getting everyone involved to ensure that the best thinking is available for solving the problem. Reminding the team of this principle helps encourage members to express ideas more freely and to blend and combine their ideas. It thus helps the team generate new, creative solutions that none of the members could have developed alone.

3. **Write It Up**. Whenever complex concepts are being discussed in a meeting, ask someone to write down the key elements of each concept. For example, if someone states a proposal, ask him or her to write it on the board to make sure it is stated in a way that all the members understand. Or if members express multiple concerns about a proposal, ask someone to list the concerns on a chart pad. It is also important to write up the final proposal once the team reaches consensus, to make sure that all the "tweaks" are accurately recorded.

4. **Turning Language Around.** Sometimes team members express comments that sound critical of others' ideas or of the team process. As facilitator you can honor their viewpoints while smoothing the path to consensus by rephrasing the comments to emphasize their positive aspects. For example, someone might say, "Here we go again! They're asking us to do more with no support." At this point the facilitator could comment something like, "Yes, it's important to discuss what support people need before we move forward."

5. **Ring Jai.** This is a Japanese concept, signifying a felt sense that a team is at consensus on a proposal. Simply saying, "I sense *ring jai*" rather than going through the entire process that a given tool involves can help move the team forward quickly.

6. **Moving Forward.** Work teams cycle through many ups, downs, and periods when not much is happening. You can help the team stay focused by emphasizing that "we're going to move forward" and using tools that foster forward movement.

7. **One on One.** During a meeting you might sense that one member has a concern or an idea that he or she has not clearly expressed, or that this person's behavior is bothering others. If your hunch is strong or it persists for some time, you might want to ask that individual to meet with

you privately one on one, explaining that your intention is to help the team function more harmoniously.

8. **Disappearing Task Force** *(DTF)*. When a complex task needs to be carried out, suggest that a DTF be set up. A DTF involves two or more team members who meet to accomplish a specific purpose. When the task is accomplished the task force disbands.

9. **Pyramiding Out.** This strategy, designed to foster widespread ownership of the proposals that the work team wants to put into action, is shown in figure 4. Each member of the team (the Xs around the circle) agrees to get feedback on the proposal from a larger entity to which that member belongs (the pyramid to which each X is connected).

Figure 4

Pyramiding Out

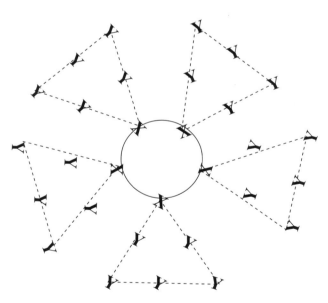

O	=	Work team
X	=	Team members
△	=	Larger entities to which various team members belong
Y	=	Other members of the larger entities with whom team members share team proposals

10. **Collective Consensus.** Sometimes you work with a team for only a limited time or on a fairly straightforward task (for example, leading a weekend workshop). It is still worthwhile to initially spend some time ensuring smooth team functioning. One way to accomplish this is to ask team members to articulate what they need from you. If the resulting list of needs seems reasonable, indicate that you will treat it as a "collective consensus," meaning that you plan to address all their requests without going through a formal consensus-building process.

11. **Circle Relay.** Circle relay is a method for making sure that the voice of every member of the team has been heard with respect to the issue now being discussed. It simply means suggesting that after the first person has spoken the next person will speak and so forth, until all have had a chance to speak. If the team is not sitting in a circle you can adjust to fit the situation, for example, "We'll hear first from the people in this row, then from the people in the next row, and so on."

12. **Shorten the Runway.** When people feel intensely about an issue, they sometimes want to tell the whole story, so they tend to start speaking faster and give a lot of detail, causing listeners to wonder, "What's the point?" Like an airplane, they can coast for a long time on the ground, but they really haven't left the airport yet. Asking an individual who has the floor to "shorten the runway" reminds him to take off, stay on track, and say what's most important, in a brief time frame that allows more time for others' sharing. For introducing us to this concept we want to thank Mark Milleman, the external consultant who co-leads the ContinUO executive institute for educational leaders sponsored by the University of Oregon's College of Education.

13. **Group Whine.** People may feel frustrated about some aspect of the issue that the team is facing. As a result, they may not be able to focus on moving forward but instead keep returning to their gripes. If you sense that this is happening you can call for a "group whine," setting time for about five minutes and allowing people to voice their frustrations freely, then asking them to return their focus to moving the team forward.

14. **Bracketing**. If team members appear to be having trouble staying focussed on the topic, you can ask them to "bracket" their other concerns for now. Have them imagine putting a screen, or drawing a big line, between the topic being discussed and everything else they have on their minds. If people continue to bring up other ideas, you can write them down on a sheet called something like "Other Concerns," saying, "We'll put that on a list, and we can address it later." For other ideas to help maintain team focus, we recommend the book *Dimensions of Thinking* by Robert Marzano and his colleagues (1988).

15. **Hopes and Concerns**. When considering any change, participants usually have both hopes for what the change will accomplish and concerns about what the change might bring. Reflecting on both hopes and concerns helps a team consider the possible changes that might need to be considered in deciding whether, or how, to implement a proposal. *Hopes* involve the positives that the team wants to accomplish by implementing the proposal, while *concerns* are expectations of possible negatives that might occur (Schmuck, 1997). For example, if teachers plan more use of cooperative learning strategies, a hope might be that students will increase their learning through social interaction. A concern might be that some students will do all the work while the others coast.

16. **Plus-Minus-Interesting**. A simple way to help team members reflect on their feelings about a proposal or idea is to ask them to rate it as Plus, Minus, or Interesting. Unlike Tool 8, *Ask Yes-No-What Do You Need?*, which requires members to take a definite stand for or against the proposal, this procedure lets participants express themselves in a more tentative, and hence less risky, fashion. Team members can simply indicate whether they are leaning towards (Plus) or away from (Minus) the proposal. They can also defer from expressing either a positive or negative feeling by opting for a neutral (Interesting) position. This technique is taken from the CoRT Thinking model of teaching (De Bono, 1986).

17. **Other Point of View**. Many social scientists believe that each individual has an operating state that determines, and thus limits, his or her interpre-

tations of the world. Other Point of View reminds team members to suspend their own judgment and try to see issues from the perspectives of other members. This process helps members commit to a compromise that allows them to maintain their own viewpoint but at the same time take others' views into account. The metaphor for OPV is "walk a mile in my shoes." It reflects the idea that after you've considered a situation from another person's perspective, you have a much better idea of what their journey has been.

Tool Card Masters

Following this page you will find a set of tool card masters. Each explains the conditions under which a specific tool is called for and the process for using it. We recommend that you use these masters to make a photocopy set of the tool cards for each member of the teams with which you are working. We suggest making copies on stiff cover stock to ensure the tool cards' durability.

You will notice that some cards have print on both sides, so be sure to copy the back material on the back of the card containing the front material. If you make your photocopies on standard 8-1/2" X 11" sheets, we recommend that you cut the tool cards in half, to a 5-1/2" X 8-1/2" size, which is the same size as the set of tool cards provided for the team leader in the envelope at the back of the Toolkit.

Tools
in the Toolkit

	Location in the Toolkit
Phase I. Laying the Groundwork	
Tool 1, *State a Purpose*	pages 7-9
Tool 2, *Set Group Agreements*	pages 11-14
Tool 3, *Develop a Common Knowledge Base*	pages 15-16
Tool 4, *Clarify Consensus*	pages 17-21
Tool 5, *Form Kaleidoscope Groups*	pages 23-24
Phase II. Working toward Consensus	
Tool 6, *Fly the Helicopter Higher: Focus on Big Ideas*	pages 29-30
Tool 7, *Float a Trial Balloon*	pages 31-32
Tool 8, *Ask Yes-No-What Do You Need?*	pages 33-35
Tool 9, *Brainstorm From → To*	pages 37-38
Tool 10, *Listen for a Breakthrough*	pages 39-43
Tool 11, *Call for a Power Sweep*	pages 45-46
Tool 12, *Do a Five-Finger Share*	pages 47-50
Tool 13, *Take a Backup Vote*	pages 51-53
Tool 14, *Test for Critical Mass*	pages 55-56
Phase III. Moving into Action	
Tool 15, *Cluster Idea Cards*	pages 59 -60
Tool 16, *Spend Your Dots*	pages 61-62
Tool 17, *Develop an Action Timeline*	pages 63-64

The Complete Toolkit for Building High-Performance Work Teams

Nancy Golden and Joyce P. Gall • **ERIC** Clearinghouse on Educational Management • University of Oregon

Setting Priorities on the Goals of a Team Meeting

1. To help members stay on task, list the varied goals that they are trying to accomplish, and note those that differ sufficiently on a chart pad.

2. By rating each goal from 1 (low) to 5 (high) on both its urgency and its importance, team members set priorities and maintain team focus.

   a. The *importance* of a particular goal signifies how critical it is to achievement of the team's overall purpose.

   b. The *urgency* of a particular goal signifies how critical it is that the goal be achieved now instead of later.

3. The importance and urgency scores provided by each team member are added together and the total score for each goal is calculated.

State a Purpose

What: *State a Purpose* is a process to help the team clarify its specific goal and the priorities that determine its focus.

When: Use *State a Purpose* at the first team meeting to help all team members start their work together "on the same page," and at subsequent meetings to help team members focus on their most important priorities at particular points in time.

Why: Often members bring very different assumptions and goals to a work team. This process helps to ensure that the team has enough common ground to blend or choose among those goals as it carries out its work.

Process for Stating a Purpose

1. At the initial team meeting point out that being clear and specific about the team's purpose helps keep team members on track and helps the team achieve its purpose in a timely way.

2. Give examples of the specific purpose of work teams with which you have been affiliated (e.g., to develop a school program to reduce student failure), or of individual team meetings (e.g., to review school data on student dropout rates).

3. Ask members to share their views as to the team's overall purpose. If there is disagreement you may wish to use **Tool 6,** *Fly the Helicopter Higher* or **Tool 8,** *Ask Yes-No-What Do You Need?* to achieve consensus on the team's purpose.

4. At each subsequent meeting, ask someone to state the purpose of the meeting, that is, the outcome to be achieved by the end of the meeting that indicates the meeting was effective.

2 Set Group Agreements

What: Setting group agreements is a process for clarifying the general behavior that team members can count on from each other, and establishing the ground rules for how the team will make decisions and handle conflict.

When: If possible, set group agreements at the first team meeting.

Why: A team functions much more comfortably and efficiently if members understand what they can expect and what is expected of them.

Process for Setting Group Agreements

1. During team meetings people should feel free to take care of their personal needs, like getting a cup of coffee or using the restroom. Suggest that everyone agree to follow the 21-year-old rule, that is, "We're all adults, and we'll act that way" in taking care of personal needs in a way that minimizes disruptions to the meeting.

2. Ask members to brainstorm a list of the characteristics of the ineffective meetings they've attended, and write it on chart pack paper. Then ask them to list the characteristics of effective meetings.

3. Using the lists as a basis, ask team members to volunteer ideas for specific agreements needed to ensure effective team functioning. You may wish to suggest topics to address (e.g., attendance, agenda, minutes, meeting tasks, tasks between meetings, decision-making, handling conflict).

4. Coach the members who introduce ideas to say precisely what they need from the group, and how agreement about it will promote individuals' comfort and the team's effectiveness. If no one says anything contradictory, you can accept all these needs as group agreements.

5. In cases of disagreement, have members discuss differing viewpoints. You may wish to use one or more of the tools from Phase II, Working toward Consensus, to help the team reach consensus on group agreements.

6. Ask someone to type up the group agreements and make copies for each team member. Emphasize that you expect all team members to follow all the group agreements, and if they want to change any of them in the future to bring it up for discussion at a future meeting.

7. In subsequent meetings, if you sense someone is not following the group agreements, remind team members of the relevant agreement and their commitment to follow it.

Develop a Common Knowledge Base

What: Developing a common knowledge base is a process for ensuring that all team members have access to necessary information to address the issue with which the team is dealing.

When: Developing a common knowledge base should be done soon after the first team meeting.

Why: A team is more effective when its members start "on the same page" with respect to their knowledge about the issue they plan to address. Developing a common knowledge base based on the education literature provides team members with the "big picture." It also helps the team focus on facts and data, not merely opinions and feelings.

Process for Developing the Knowledge Base

1. Team members brainstorm the common knowledge that they need as a basis for achieving their purpose and summarize ideas on a chart pad.

2. Team members identify possible sources of information or agree to identify sources by the next meeting.

3. Someone on the team gets copies of the key sources to all team members.

4. If there is not too much information, all team members read it before the next meeting. If there is a lot of information, they use the jigsaw method, giving each team member a different section to read and summarize at the next team meeting.

5. In some cases the team may decide it needs to view a video, visit a school site, or obtain information from some other source. If so, volunteers make the necessary arrangements.

Nancy Golden and Joyce P. Gall • **ERIC** Clearinghouse on Educational Management • University of Oregon

4 Clarify Consensus

What: Consensus means that members are sufficiently in favor of a decision that no one will become an obstacle to carrying it out.

When: Clarify consensus when you sense that the team needs to agree on a specific decision or plan of action so that it can move forward.

Why: Team members' support and ownership of ideas is necessary for them to be implemented. Clarifying consensus helps guide team members toward creating that support and ownership.

Operational Definition of Consensus

The following definition is based on the booklet "A Workshop for Convenors." (Eugene Cadre, 1999).

1. All participants contribute, encourage the expression of varied opinions, and view differences as a strength rather than a hindrance.

2. Everyone understands the issue and is able to paraphrase it.

3. Consensus does not mean that the decision gives everyone his or her choice; rather, it means that members sufficiently favor the decision that no one sabotages it or tries to block carrying it out.

4. All share in the final decision; if consensus is not reached, the discussion is automatically recycled to bring more information to bear.

Illustration of Consensus

Consensus is illustrated in figure 1. It shows a group of team members (the X's around the outer circle), each of whom holds a somewhat different position from all the other members of the team. Consensus is represented by the smaller circle in the center. Consensus does not represent perfect agreement (the dot in the middle of the smaller circle), but rather a blend of, and reduced range of, perspectives on which all the members are able to reach agreement.

Figure 1 Consensus

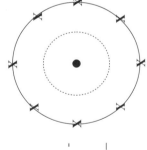

——— = Original position of each team member (X)

- - - - - = Consensus

● = Perfect agreement

Guidelines for Moving Toward Consensus

DO present your position logically and provide information to support it.
DO consider other positions carefully before you press your point.
DO acknowledge other positions that have objective and logical bases.
DO explore reasons for differences of opinion.
DO look at alternatives.
DO distinguish between objective data and gut-level feelings about an issue.
DO poll the group often, using **Tool 6,** *Listen for a Breakthrough*, and **Tool 9,** *Ask Yes-No-What Do You Need?*
DO accept "Pass" as a response, but remind members that unless they take a position their views will not be reflected in the team decision.
DON'T argue for your position without any justification.
DON'T argue automatically for your own personal priorities.
DON'T change your mind just to avoid conflict.
DON'T assume that stalemate reflects a win-lose situation.
To emphasize: Consensus does not mean that you get exactly what YOU want. It means that every team member listens to others and tries to formulate a proposal that combines many people's ideas and is agreeable to all.

The Value of Consensus

"Benjamin Franklin on Consensus" helps teams grasp the value of consensus.

1. Each team member can read the section individually.

2. Then team members pair up in kaleidoscope groups (see Tool 5) and discuss the reading selection.

3. The team comes back together, and someone from each pair volunteers to summarize their key learnings about consensus.

4.

The small groups should end their discussions in time to do a Round Robin (also known as a Power Sweep; see Tool 11). This involves asking, "How does everyone feel about the idea (or topic/issue/goal/proposal) at this point? What else would you like to know about it before you feel ready to work on it?" Give each team member a chance to respond briefly.

---

5 Form Kaleidoscope Groups

What: Kaleidoscope groups are a means to get people with different perspectives together to talk.

When: Kaleidoscope groups should be used when it is important for team members to understand multiple perspectives.

Why: People often get stuck in their own beliefs, seeing situations or proposals only from their own perspectives. They often need help to see the multiple perspectives that may exist about the issue being considered.

Process for Forming Kaleidoscope Groups

1. The metaphor of kaleidoscope groups can be explained like this:

"When you look into a kaleidoscope, you see many different pieces of glass of many different colors and shapes. Yet they come together into a beautiful design. In much the same way, when a group of people come together as a work team, each one brings his or her own perspective. However, if each team member can understand and respect multiple perspectives, the team is more likely to be able to bring those perspectives together into a powerful proposal that can be supported by the group—that is, a consensus."

2. In order for the group to begin to understand multiple perspectives, members need to interact with people they don't know well, or who have different jobs and different interests. Ask team members to pair up with someone they don't know well, someone who has a different job, or someone with different interests related to the issue on which the team plans to work.

3. The members in each small group can take 5 to 10 minutes to discuss their positions on the team issue. Suggest that they look for the similarities in their positions as well as discussing their differences.

Fly the Helicopter Higher: Focus on Big Ideas

What: *Fly the Helicopter Higher* is a process for helping team members focus on big ideas rather than on specific details when considering proposals for action.

When: Use *Fly the Helicopter Higher* when you sense team members are focusing on specific details surrounding an issue and losing sight of their common purpose as a result.

Why: Teams often disagree or fall apart because they get hung up on specific details rather than attending to the big ideas that serve their purpose and how to realize those ideas. *Fly the Helicopter Higher* helps team members refocus on big ideas.

The Process of Flying the Helicopter Higher

1. The facilitator should note points during the discussion of a proposal when one or more members appear to be focusing on, or arguing about, very specific details.

2. Point out that team agreement on such fine details is unlikely, because of the diversity of viewpoints that the team represents.

3. Ask the team to "fly the helicopter a little higher," that is, to focus on the big ideas.

Nancy Golden and Joyce P. Gall • ERIC Clearinghouse on Educational Management • University of Oregon

Float a Trial Balloon

What: Floating a trial balloon is used to ensure that team members will respond with positive comments when a new idea is introduced.

When: A trial balloon is used when a new idea is introduced and you want the team to focus on the positives of the idea before considering the negatives.

Why: Some people greet almost any new idea with negative comments, which represents the "shoot-it-down" syndrome. Team members may stop bringing up new ideas because of their fear of having them shot down. Floating a trial balloon blocks the shoot-it-down syndrome.

The Process of Floating a Trial Balloon

1. When a team member has a new idea to propose, he or she introduces it to the team.

2. For ten minutes, only positive comments about the idea are accepted and recorded on a chart pad. If anyone starts to raise questions or express concerns that reflect negatively on the proposal, remind the team that only positive comments are appropriate now, and that they will have an opportunity to ask clarifying questions or express concerns later.

3. After ten minutes, the team gets equal time to ask clarifying questions or to express concerns.

4. Ask everyone to listen to all the comments to see if there is a way to state the proposal in a form that will get them to consensus. Remind team members to "shorten the runway" (see Top Tip #12) when it is their turn so that there is time to hear from everyone.

5. When everyone has shared their ideas, ask if any of the team members can generate a proposal that may get them to consensus, or generate a proposal yourself.

6. Use Tool 11 to call for a power sweep before ending the meeting. This involves going around the room again so that each team member can say how he or she feels about the proposal at this point.

Nancy Golden and Joyce P. Gall • **ERIC** Clearinghouse on Educational Management • University of Oregon

Ask Yes-No-
What Do You Need?

What: To help a team move toward consensus, this process clarifies which team members support a proposal and what team members who do not support the proposal would need in order to support it (or an alternative proposal to which all can agree).

When: Use *Ask Yes-No-What Do You Need?* when you sense that the team is approaching consensus on a particular proposal and you want to clarify what team members who are not in support would need in order to support it.

Why: To reach consensus, team members who do not support a proposal must be given the opportunity to state what they would need in order to support it. The information they provide is then used by all team members to modify the proposal in such a way that everyone can accept it (that is, reach consensus).

The Ask Yes-No-What Do You Need? Process

1. Someone states the proposal and it is written on a chart pad.

2. Each member states either:

   a. Yes, I support the proposal, and (if he or she wishes) why, **OR**

   b. No, I don't support the proposal, and this is what I would need in order to support it.

3. The Yes/No responses are tallied on a chart (see the example that follows), with a summary of what people responding No would need in order to support the proposal. If people responding Yes also express needs, record their responses as Yes but also record what they say they need.

4. This process does not constitute a vote for or against the proposal at this point. When the chart is filled in, all team

---

members look at the data in the "I need" row and think of how the original proposal could be modified in a way that will help the team move toward consensus.

5. If the team still cannot reach consensus after trying multiple proposals, the facilitator could try using **Tool 13,** *Take a Backup Vote,* or **Tool 14,** *Test for Critical Mass.*

Brainstorm From → To

What: *Brainstorm From → To* allows team members to compare the past and future with respect to a particular phenomenon.

When: Use the *Brainstorm From → To* process when you want team members to reflect on and discuss how a particular phenomenon has changed over time.

Why: Brainstorming future scenarios helps team members envision the future and create desired changes, and reflecting on how much change has already occurred helps them stay open to moving forward.

The Brainstorm From → To Process

1. For teams with more than six members, divide the team into two or more smaller groups.

2. Each group draws a line down the middle of a piece of chart-pad paper and labels the left side FROM and the right side TO.

3. Each group reflects on a particular phenomenon. You can assign topics or let groups pick their topics. A humorous example about life for baby boomers (that is, people born in the U.S. between 1946 and 1950) and an example concerning parent-school communication follow.

4. Each group summarizes on its sheet the changes that have occurred in the phenomenon it is considering by recording specific examples of what the phenomenon was like at some point in the past (FROM) and what it is like today or what they want it to become in the future (TO).

Listen for a Breakthrough

What: *Listen for a Breakthrough* is a process that encourages members to listen to one another's ideas with respect, empathy, and openness, continuing to modify a proposal until all members' key needs are met.

When: Sometimes teams have difficulty identifying all the needs of members who vote No during the use of **Tool 8**, *Ask Yes-No-What Do You Need?* If that occurs, use *Listen for a Breakthrough*, which encourages all members voting No to clarify what they would need in order to get to Yes.

Why: For team members to work well together and make appropriate proposals, they must listen respectfully to each other's ideas and consider a whole range of ways of dealing with issues.

Process of Listening for a Breakthrough

1. Explain that to reach consensus, each team member must be willing to move from his or her position toward the position of members with different perspectives. The breakthrough for which they must listen is a way to modify the proposal so that the team can reach consensus.

2. After one team member has expressed his or her perspective, do a listening check, perhaps by engaging in the following exercise: "Everyone take out a sheet of paper and write down what Joe just said." Have team members compare what they wrote, and note who paraphrased Joe's statement most accurately.

3. Explain that the kind of listening required for an effective work team involves more than being able to paraphrase what others say, though that is important. Team members also must listen with *empathy*, which means putting yourself mentally and emotionally in someone else's place so completely that you know what it feels like to walk in the other person's shoes.

4. The idea of moving toward other members' perspectives is illustrated in figure 2. It is the same as the consensus circle (figure 1) in **Tool 4**, *Clarify Consensus*, except that figure 2 shows each team member (the X's around the outer circle) moving closer to other members' perspectives (the arrows pointing inward). The process of moving closer

is accomplished by looking for common themes and seeking a blend, or reduced range, of perspectives on which all the members can reach consensus.

5. Remind the team that the "breakthrough" for which they must listen is how to modify a proposal to take into account the needs of all members. Also point out the principal of synergy, or $1 + 1 = 3$, meaning that a proposal that builds on the ideas of all team members is usually superior to a proposal suggested by one member, because all members enrich it.

6. Team members respond to each suggested proposal modification either with Yes or No. If a member's position is still No, the member should identify what they would need to move to Yes.

7. Continue this process until the team appears ready to accept by consensus the latest modification of the proposal. If consensus still is not reached, you might want to try **Tool 13**, *Take a Backup Vote*, giving any remaining members still at No a chance to stand aside so that the team can move forward.

8. Sometimes this process takes the team in a different direction from the one in which it was heading before. The breakthrough might be a very different proposal from what most of the team members were favoring previously, but one that they can all support. For example, a high school teacher who taught creative writing was struggling with the issue of how to get students to do more writing in order to increase their writing skills. Most teachers' ideas for dealing with this concern are fairly traditional, like giving students more written assignments or asking parents to help their children write letters. The creative writing teacher came up with a breakthrough idea. He told his students that for the next 18 weeks he would not speak in class, but would deliver all his communications in written form. The teacher reported that "Each day in class brought greater student input.... If I was talking less and writing more, they could talk less and write more" (Ryan, 1991).

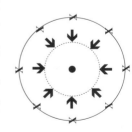

**Figure 2
Moving Toward Consensus**

●	= Original position of each team member (X)
→	= Moving closer to other members' perspectives
—	= Consensus
- - -	= Perfect agreement

Call for a Power Sweep

What: *Call for a Power Sweep* involves asking every team member to take a turn expressing his or her feelings about the idea or proposal that the team is considering.

When: Use *Call for a Power Sweep* when a proposal has been generated and you want the team to listen to each member's feelings and ideas about the proposal.

Why: Getting everyone's input provides synergy (see Top Tip #2). By moving the proposal beyond one person to a concept in which all the members share, the team can see that the whole is greater than the sum of its parts: 1 + 1 = 3. This increases the opportunity for the team to reach consensus.

The Process of Calling for a Power Sweep

1. State that it is now a good time for all team members to share their ideas and feelings about the idea or proposal in order to help the team move toward consensus.

2. Go around the room and invite each member to share, asking them to keep their comments brief and on the topic.

Nancy Golden and Joyce P. Gall • **ERIC** Clearinghouse on Educational Management • University of Oregon

Do a Five-Finger Share

What: *Five-Finger Share* lets each team member show how he or she feels about a proposal by holding up one to five fingers.

When: Use *Five-Finger Share* to see if the team is at or near consensus, which represents all members voting 3, 4, or 5 on the proposal.

Why: A *Five-Finger Share* allows the team to quickly sense the level of support for a proposal.

What each number represents:

Five fingers: Love—I support the idea and will work actively to help it become a reality.

Four fingers: Really like—I support the idea; while I may not be a major player, I will do what is appropriate.

Three fingers: Neutral—I'm not opposed to the idea; I don't care if others want to do it; I won't undermine their efforts.

Two fingers: Really dislike—I prefer other options. While I dislike the proposal, I will abide by the decision of the group for at least a trial period of time and I will not "sabotage" the decision.

One finger: Hate—I am opposed to the idea.

The Five-Finger Share process:

1. Figure 3 is a more detailed version of figure 1, Consensus, from **Tool 4**, *Clarify Consensus*. It represents an agreement target, which is similar in design to a dart board. The outermost circle (1) represents one finger; the next circle in (2) represents two fingers; and the next three circles in all represent consensus, that is, sufficient team agreement to move the proposal forward, with the third circle in (3) representing three fingers, the fourth circle in representing four fingers, and the fifth circle in representing five fingers. Note that three fingers corresponds to the line representing consensus in figure 1, while five fingers corresponds to the point representing perfect agreement in figure

---

1. Reproduce the target on the board or a chart pad before stating the proposal to be considered, and make a mark on the target for each team member's position.

2. Each team member raises one to five fingers to indicate how he or she feels about the proposal.

3. If everyone in the group raises three, four, or five fingers, consensus has been reached.

4. If any team members raise just one or two fingers, each of them states what they would need before they could raise three, four, or five fingers.

5. If some team members raise one or two fingers, try **Tool 10**, *Listen for a Breakthrough*, to help the team reach consensus.

6. Sometimes a team cannot reach consensus after trying multiple proposals. In that case, use **Tool 13**, *Take a Backup Vote*, or **Tool 14**, *Test for Critical Mass*, to determine whether there is sufficient agreement to move forward.

7. If consensus still is not reached, the leader can ask members who still are at one or two fingers if they are willing to stand aside, which they can indicate by holding one finger sideways rather than pointed up. By standing aside, a member declares willingness not to block the proposal from being accepted in order to allow the team to move forward.

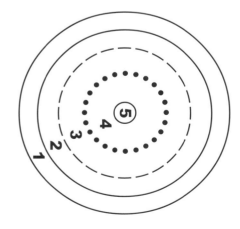

Figure 3
Agreement Target

Take a Backup Vote

What: A backup vote is a vote to determine whether a proposal has enough support to move forward.

When: A backup vote is used when the team has not reached consensus. It is more precise than using **Tool 14,** *Test for Critical Mass.*

Why: Taking a backup vote provides a way for the team to move forward by revealing whether the majority of team members support the proposal.

The Backup Vote Process

1. A team member needs to clearly state the proposal; it is helpful to write it on a chart pad as well.

2. Other team members may ask only clarifying questions concerning the proposal. This is not the time to reopen a debate or make statements as to why the proposal might not work.

3. Generally a quorum is necessary to take a backup vote. A quorum means that a majority of team members (that is, one more than half) must be present. If a quorum is not present, you will probably have to table the proposal until the next meeting.

4. Each team member votes either to support or reject the proposal. If a majority of those present (that is, one more than half) accept the proposal, the backup vote is positive and the team can move forward on the proposal.

5. Ask each of the members who voted to reject the proposal if they want to stand aside. This means that, while they are still not in favor of the proposal, they agree not to block it from being accepted and to allow the team to move forward.

6. What happens if you suspect that some team members might miss a meeting to prevent the team from having a quorum?

   a. Arrange the time and location of team meetings to suit as many team members' schedules as possible, and announce future meetings well in advance.

   b. Make clear that group agreements specify that all team members agree to attend each meeting.

   c. Track who is not at the meeting, and talk to absent members about their nonattendance before the next meeting.

   d. Assume that people rarely miss meetings intentionally, but that circumstances sometimes prevent individuals from attending meetings.

Test for Critical Mass

What: Critical mass is the approximate number of team members who must support a proposal for it to be implemented. Not a precise number, it represents the facilitator's sense that there is enough support for the proposal to make it likely to succeed.

When: Test for critical mass when the team has not reached consensus but you sense that there might be sufficient support for a proposal to implement it.

Why: Implementation of new ideas is often difficult. You need to determine if there are enough "cheerleaders" behind an idea to make it go. They represent critical mass.

Guidelines for Determining the Number of Team Members Needed for Critical Mass

1. It is up to the facilitator to sense when the number of team members in support of a proposal indicates critical mass. This judgment is not precise but only approximate, and depends on the team "feel."

2. Generally, the smaller the total number of team members, the higher the number (that is, the proportion of members) necessary for critical mass. Conversely, the larger the total number of team members, the lower the number (that is, the proportion of members) necessary for critical mass.

3. In some situations, critical mass depends on not only the number of team members who are in support of a proposal, but also the particular team members who support it. For example, some members may be key stakeholders with respect to a particular proposal, while acceptance of the proposal will have less impact on other members who are not key stakeholders. In this case, you might sense that critical mass was not present unless at least a majority of members from the key-stakeholder group support the proposal.

The Complete Toolkit for Building High-Performance Work Teams

Nancy Golden and Joyce P. Gall • **ERIC** Clearinghouse on Educational Management • University of Oregon

Cluster Idea Cards

What: Clustering idea cards allows a team to organize a large number of ideas concerning an issue.

When: Have the team write and cluster idea cards whenever it needs to pull together a lot of information and ideas to help clarify its future direction.

Why: There are times when large amounts of information need to be synthesized for the team's review as a guide to moving forward.

The Process of Clustering Idea Cards

1. Using 3" x 5" note cards (or post-it notes), team members list ideas concerning the issue being considered, writing each idea on a separate card, front side only. So that the cards can be easily read, ask members to state each idea briefly and print it in large, dark print.

2. If the team has more than six members, break it into two or more groups. Each group takes a stack of idea cards and clusters them by putting together the ideas that have something in common.

3. Team members give each cluster of idea cards a name representing the big concept of what all the ideas in that cluster have in common, and write the name for each cluster on a separate card. For example, a team might be considering a proposal to extend the school year for two weeks. It might find that some ideas have to do with fears about the effects on parents, and other ideas are related to concerns about financing a longer school year.

4. The members of each group take a final look at the cards in each cluster to see if any clusters should be combined or renamed, if any cards should be moved, or if any new clusters are needed.

5. To help the team focus on the ideas most relevant to its purpose, you might first want to review **Tool 1,** *State a Purpose.* It might also help to first review **Tool 6,** *Fly the Helicopter Higher,* to remind team members to focus on big ideas.

The Complete Toolkit for Building High-Performance Work Teams

Nancy Golden and Joyce P. Gall • **ERIC** Clearinghouse on Educational Management • University of Oregon

Spend Your Dots

What: *Spend Your Dots* allows a team to prioritize ideas for action by revealing members' level of support for various idea clusters.

When: When it is important to determine the team's top priorities, have the team spend its dots using equal distribution. When it is important for each team member to be able to express the intensity of his or her preferences, have the team spend its dots using weighted distribution.

Why: For the team to reach consensus, you need to help members set priorities. This process allows the team to set priorities in a fair and nonthreatening manner

The Spend-Your-Dots Process

1. Depending on the number of idea card clusters that need to be prioritized, each team member receives the same number of self-stick dots (or post-it notes).

2. Team members use their dots to prioritize.

   a. For equal distribution, each member puts each of his or her dots on the name card for a different cluster of idea cards. A member can put only one dot on each name card.

   b. For weighted distribution, each member puts each of his or her dots on the name card for one *or more* specific clusters of idea cards. A member can put anywhere from one to the total number of dots on a particular name card.

3. After all dots have been applied, the name cards with the most dots are the top-priority items.

The Complete Toolkit for Building High-Performance Work Teams

Nancy Golden and Joyce P. Gall • ERIC Clearinghouse on Educational Management • University of Oregon

Develop an Action Timeline

What: *Develop an Action Timeline* involves putting the actions that the team identifies as high priority in the order of what needs to happen first, second, third, and so forth. After team members agree on the sequence of actions, they also specify (for example, by month) when they want each action to be completed.

When: Use *Develop an Action Timeline* when the team is ready to develop a long-term plan of action.

Why: People need a place to begin. This process allows the team to break its planned tasks into small parts so that it can get get started.

The Process of Developing an Action Timeline

1. After the team has completed categorizing, naming, and prioritizing each group of idea cards (see Tools 15 and 16), ask the team to put the name cards for each group of cards that involve high-priority actions in order of what needs to happen first, second, third, and so forth.

2. Once they have put all the name cards in order, ask members to indicate for each card when they want each action completed. See the example of a school's action timeline for developing a school improvement plan.

3. Once the name cards have been ordered and dated, have the timeline typed up so that it can serve as a step-by-step guide for, and provide benchmarks toward, achieving tasks.

References

Conley, D. T. & Goldman, P. (1994). *Facilitative leadership: How principals lead without doiminating.* Eugene, OR: Oregon School Study Council.

De Bono, E. (1986). *CoRT thinking teacher's notes: Creativity.* New York: Pergamon.

Eugene Cadre (1999). *A workshop for convenors.* Eugene, OR: Eugene School District 4J.

Fullan, M. G. & Stiegelbauer, S. (1991). *The new meaning of educational change.* New York: Teachers College Press.

Golden, N. (1994). *Techniques to build high performing work teams.* Albany, OR: Greater Albany Public Schools.

Marzano, R. J.; R. S. Brandt; C. S. Hughes; B. F. Jones; B. Z. Presseisen; S. C. Rankin; C. Suhor; and M. Knoll (1988). *Dimensions of thinking: A framework for curriculum and instruction.* Alexandria, VA: Association for Supervision and Curriculum Development.

Patterson, J. L. (1993). *Leadership for tomorrow's schools.* Alexandria, VA: Association for Supervision and Curriculum Developoment.

Ryan, P. M. (1991). Whose voice do you hear? An experiment in nonverbal communication. *The Teacher.* (September), 32.

Schmuck, R. A. (1997). *Practical action research.* Arlington Heights, IL: IRI Skylight.

Recommended Reading

Conley, D. T., & Goldman, P. (1994). *Facilitative leadership: How principals lead without dominating*. Eugene, OR: Oregon School Study Council. The authors describe the nature of facilitative leadership and its implications for the design and operation of leadership in schools.

Doyle, M. & Straus, D. (1976). *How to make meetings work*. New York: Jove Books. This book provides guidelines and a set of tools for both meeting leaders and meeting participants to improve the procedures and productivity of meetings. It is based on the Interaction Method, which defines four roles that need to be carried out to improve a meeting's functioning: the facilitator, the recorder, the group member, and the manager/chairperson. The book includes a chapter laying out 62 tools for solving problems in groups, for example, What's the "Real" Problem?, Whose Problem Is It, Anyway?, and Energizing the Group.

Hoffman, C. & Ness, J. (1998). *Putting sense into consensus: Solving the puzzle of making team decisions*. Tacoma, WA: VISTA Associates. This book describes four "cornerpieces" in the puzzle of consensus: Why use consensus, What is consensus, When do you use consensus, and How do you reach consensus. The book provides questions and activities laid out in a set of steps for determining each part of the consensus puzzle. It also includes a variety of process tools for helping a team work toward consensus.

Hoyle, J. R., English, F. W., & Steffy, B. E. (1998). *Skills for successful 21st century school leaders*. Arlington, VA: American Association of School Administrators. The authors propose standards for peak performers and lay out skills, readings, and activities for skill mastery in ten key aspects of school leadership. The chapters on visionary leadership, policy and governance, communication and community relations, and staff development are particularly relevant to the building of effective work teams.

Patterson, J. L. (1993). *Leadership for tomorrow's schools*. Alexandria, VA: Association for Supervision and Curriculum Development. Written by a school superintendent, this book provides a clear conception of how leadership is being changed by and is changing organizational realities in the workplace. Includes guidelines for building consensus and tools for reaching group decisions, which formed the basis for some of the tools in this Toolkit.

Recommended Reading

Schmuck, R. A., & Runkel, P. J. (1994). *Handbook of organization development in schools and colleges* (4th ed.). Prospect Heights, IL: Waveland. ERIC Document Reference No. ED 386 817. Designed to help educators at every level bring about constructive organizational change in their work settings, the book explains how to create more positive human-interaction patterns derived from behavioral science. The book includes numerous exercises and activities that work teams can use to improve their organizational structure, process, and outcomes.

Smith, S. C., & Piele, P. K. (Eds.). (1997). *School leadership: Handbook for excellence*. Third edition. Eugene, OR: ERIC Clearinghouse on Educational Management. The authors summarize and explain a large body of literature on the practice of school leadership. The chapters on quality work teams and on leading meetings provide useful information for building effective work teams.